Memory Quilts

20 Heartwarming Projects with Special Techniques

Memory Quilts

20 Heartwarming Projects with Special Techniques

BY SANDY BONSIB

A STONESONG PRESS BOOK

CREATIVE PUBLISHING international

Creative Publishing international, Inc.
18705 Lake Drive East
Chanhassen, Minnesota 55317
1-800-328-3895
www.creativepub.com

President/CEO: Michael Eleftheriou
Vice President/Publisher: Linda Ball
Vice President/Retail Sales: Kevin Haas
Executive Editor: Alison Brown Cerier

MEMORY QUILTS

The Stonesong Press, LLC

Publisher: Paul Fargis
Directors: Alison Fargis, Ellen Scordato
Executive Editor: Judy Pray
Copy Editor: Candie Frankel
Designer: Kay Schuckhart
Photographer: Mark Frey

Library of Congress Cataloging-in-Publication Data

Bonsib, Sandy, 1950-
    Memory quilts : 20 heartwarming projects with special techniques / by Sandy Bonsib.
        p. cm.
    "A Stonesong Press book."
    Includes bibliographical references and index.
    ISBN 1-58923-152-X (sc)
    1. Patchwork--Patterns. 2. Quilting--Patterns. 3. Transfer--printing. 4. Photographs on cloth. I. Title.
    TT835.B62824 2004
    746.46'041--dc22
                        2004010279

Printed in China.
10 9 8 7 6 5 4 3 2 1

DEDICATION

This book is dedicated to my wonderful mother-in-law, Dee Bickley, a memory maker if there ever was one. Her accomplishments are many—wife, mother, grandmother, great grandmoth-er, volunteer extraordinaire, helper and caretaker to so many and so often, marathon runner until the age of eighty-four, and still a college student at the age of ninety. She is without a doubt a most amazing woman, and it is a privilege and an honor to be her daughter-in-law.

Contents

Making a Memory Quilt

What is a memory quilt? In short, any quilt with a bit of personal or group history attached to it—and often that means literally attached. A memory quilt is a collage of collected items that, put together, have the power to trigger all sorts of pleasing memories and associations. It's a way of preserving and showcasing fabrics, photographs, paper ephemera, documents, small personal treasures, bits of lace, and any other item you can think to attach.

Photo transfer is the technique most often associated with memory quilts, but there are many other embellishment options waiting to be explored. As a quiltmaker, I love to work all sorts of additional pieces into my designs. The projects in this book will give you lots of ideas for working your own memories into the quilts you make.

CHOOSING A THEME

People make memory quilts for many reasons—to celebrate a special occasion, mark a personal milestone, remember someone special, or simply to reflect on the pleasures of everyday life. As the projects in this book show, you can make memory quilts to celebrate Grandpa's 80th birthday, welcome a new baby, or showcase the Christmas ornaments your children made when they were young. There are no limits or restrictions. Your quilts will be as unique and personal as your own reflections and memorabilia.

Subjects for memory quilts abound. Sit back, relax, and let your mind wander. Revisit old photographs and letters, or check the contents of that shoebox you have hidden in the closet. Once you decide on a theme and start collecting items, keep your eyes open for extra embellishments that will contribute to the mood and spirit of your quilt. Around the time of her own wedding, and realizing how she had followed in the footsteps of her mother, grandmother, and great-grandmother, Sue Van Gerpen began researching the women in her family, four generations in all. The resulting quilt features old photographs, antique buttons, and a lace handkerchief and textiles the family had saved. Kathy Staley used a photo transfer technique to preserve her children's artwork in fabric. The "memory" in Carolyn Vallelunga's work is old quilts themselves. Carolyn preserves what she can of quilts that are so damaged that the only other alternative would be to throw them away. Use the materials you have to make the quilts shown in this book. There are no limits to what you can make using your own memorabilia.

GROUP PROJECTS

Most quilts are made by one person working alone, but memory quilts can be particularly satisfying as group projects. Patchwork or appliqué blocks made by individual quilters can be sewn together into one quilt. Individual signature blocks let group members write personal messages that become part of the quilt's overall message or theme.

A group quilt project can be organized by one person or by a small group or committee. If you are working solo to get the project off the ground, I recommend that you ask others to help you, even with small tasks. This not only lightens your load, but it gives others some ownership and pride in the project, too. This is especially true when working with children.

To make a quilt with my Brownie troop, I began by asking the girls, ages six to nine, to decide what designs they wanted to use. I prepared the fabric squares, purchased the markers and design books, and showed them how to do the tracing. I asked several mothers to help the girls sew the blocks together, press the seams, assemble the layers, and tie the quilts. Although the other mothers were not quilters, they were able to pick up the basics quickly and help the girls. Their presence helped everything go smoothly and made the project less stressful and more fun for me, the Brownie leader. Everyone contributed and felt a part of the project and the finished product.

When adults work together on group quilts, the process is somewhat different, but asking everyone's help is still, I think, the best way for everyone to feel invested in the project. If my small quilt group cannot readily decide which blocks to make and exchange, we take a vote with paper and pencil. Each person writes yes or no about the idea or blocks in question on a small slip of paper. The voting is confidential, with no hard feelings allowed. Voting this way encourages everyone to say what she really thinks, without feeling pressured or influenced by the group.

For family quilts, there is usually one person—the "designated quilter"—who organizes the project and sees it through to completion. If your family includes several quilters, by all means collaborate and draw on one another's creativity and expertise. If you are spearheading the project on your own, do consider asking for help. If necessary, teach the simpler skills of quiltmaking to those who are interested so that they can help you. You may well find that the pleasure you receive working on a family group quilt more than makes up for the lopsided division of labor.

Quilts as Gifts

When I give quilts as gifts, I ask for the recipient's favorite color or home decor colors. I do not ask the recipient to help me choose fabrics or block designs. People who aren't quilters don't realize that every fabric doesn't need to match, that certain colors and patterns look different up close than they do at a distance, and other things that quilters learn from experience. Give yourself, as the quilter, the freedom to choose the fabrics and the block design. Stress to the recipient the advantage of relying on the quilter's knowledge and experience. After all, the quilter's knowledge and skill are part of the gift.

Photo Transfers

Photo transfer is the most popular way to incorporate photos, documents, and other images printed into your quilts—without damage to the original item. The image is printed onto fabric, and the fabric can then be cut and sewn into the quilt design.

There are several photo transfer methods, each with pros and cons. Which you choose will depend on the quality of image you desire as well as the type of computer printer or copier you own or can access. With today's sophisticated computers and copiers, you can resize, rotate, reverse, and overlap images. With a computer, you can download and copy digital pictures.

In addition to a printer or a copier, you will also need special photo transfer paper or fabric. Be sure to buy a transfer paper or fabric that is compatible with the equipment. Read and follow the manufacturer's instructions. If you are using a transfer paper or fabric for the first time, do a dry run on plain paper to test the size, orientation, and print quality.

Photo Transfer Paper and Laser Color Copier

This method produces the greatest clarity and the best color. Laser photo transfers often look as good as or better than their original photographs. You will need special photo transfer paper, a laser color copier or printer, and a heat source.

The process takes two steps. First, the image is copied in reverse onto the transfer paper. To get a reverse image, simply select the copier's "mirror image" or "reverse image" option. Then the mirror image copy is heat-transferred from the paper to the fabric. A heat press in a T-shirt shop or fabric store works best, but an iron will work with practice.

Some copiers allow you to reduce or enlarge an image, change from color to black and white, or lighten or darken the printing. If you are lucky enough to own a laser color printer, you can perform these functions on your computer.

Experiment with different transfer papers to find one you like, as the quality varies. Some transfer papers produce images that are stiff on the fabric, that cannot be ironed, or that are damaged by washing. My favorite transfer paper, chosen after comparing ten types, is Photo Transfer Paper from Martingale & Company/That Patchwork Place. It produces great color and stiffens the fabric only slightly compared to other brands. You can iron directly on the images, even when using steam and high heat.

Photo Transfer Paper and Inkjet Printer

This method requires a special photo transfer paper, an inkjet printer or copier, and a heat source. The process takes two steps. Inkjet printers apply a thin sealing coat to make their water-soluble inks permanent. The sealer gives transferred images a stiffer, heavier appearance. The resulting image lacks the clarity of a laser print, but many people still choose this method because of the convenience of using a home computer and color inkjet printer. As with laser papers, inkjet photo transfer papers vary, so it's worthwhile to test them.

Fabric Sheets and an Inkjet Printer

In this method, the image is printed directly on specially treated white cotton or muslin fabric, without having to use a transfer paper. The fabric is available in a standard size that you can feed directly into an inkjet printer or copier. A paper backing keeps the fabric stiff during the printer feed and is peeled off afterwards. With some fabric sheets, images are immediately permanent; with others, you treat the image (or pretreat the fabric) to make the image permanent. You can reduce or enlarge, change colors, and lighten or darken the images. The printer inks tend to seep down into the fabric, giving the images a soft, watery look.

SIGNATURE BLOCKS

Hand-written signature blocks can be made in two ways: by writing directly on the fabric or by using a photo transfer method. Each approach has pros and cons. Writing directly on fabric is immediate and inexpensive—as long as you don't make any mistakes. Contributors who don't quilt must be reminded to stay clear of the seam allowance. The photo transfer approach allows room for error. People can try several versions of their message on paper "blocks" and choose the best one for a photo transfer onto fabric. If a sample is too large or spills into the seam allowance, you can always reduce it to fit the block.

To write directly on fabric, choose a pen with permanent ink. Never use water-soluble ink. Even if you think a quilt will never be washed, someone may accidentally splash water on it or try to spot-clean it. Just a little wetness can cause a water-soluble ink to run and stain. Many quilting books suggest a .1mm size pen nib for quilt labels, but I find this ultra-fine tip snags the fabric and makes it difficult to write. I prefer to use the slightly wider .5mm or .8mm size. Tips in these sizes glide smoothly, allowing the writer to move easily and without hesitation. Choose the nib size that attracts attention from a distance, so viewers will move in for a closer look. When in doubt, try out a few sizes, tack your samples to the wall, and view them from across the room. Even if you can't read the writing, you want to be able to tell that the blocks are not blank. You can use the same size nibs for writing on paper.

To prevent shifting as you write, set the fabric on a sheet of fine-grit #400 wet-dry black sandpaper. Some people tape the fabric to the table instead, but the fabric may fray when the tape is removed. If fraying has been a problem for you, try a low-tack tape or switch to the sandpaper backing.

EMBELLISHMENT TECHNIQUES

There are many options besides photo transfers and signature blocks for decorating memory quilts. Don't say no to a particular embellishment just because you think it's too big, too heavy, or too delicate to use. With the right know-how, you can attach all sorts of memorabilia.

Tacking by Hand

Tacking objects to the quilt surface with needle and thread is preferred wherever possible. A quilt is naturally soft and pliable. Hand tacking respects and works with this characteristic. Choose a thread weight and needle appropriate to the memorabilia being attached. Regular sewing thread is perfect for bits of lace, handkerchiefs, small buttons, and other lightweight items. Use pearl cotton and a chenille needle for slightly heavier pieces, such as the mortarboard in Graduation Day (page 72), the dog biscuits in Our Wonderful Lab (page 96), or the artist's brushes in A Watercolor Memory (page 92). Your stitches can be invisible or decorative.

Glue

Some objects are too heavy or awkward to stitch to the quilt surface. When an attempt to sew something in place becomes time-consuming or frustrating, consider using glue instead. All of the items in Grandma's Kitchen (page 52) are attached with glue. Straight rows were critical to the overall look of this quilt, and with a hot-glue gun, I could pinpoint the location of each object. Try different types of glues according to the memorabilia being attached. Test whether you can remove glued-on objects, if you think that will ever be an issue.

Vinyl Pockets

Clear vinyl pockets let you display photos, certificates, brochures, and postcards while protecting them. They offer an alternative to photo transfers and give the quilt a totally different look. Displaying original ephemera can give your quilt a truly historical presence.

Shop for clear vinyl at stores that sell home decorating fabrics. Vinyl is sold on rolls, like fabric, so you can buy exactly what you need. It is available in several thicknesses and is easy to cut and sew; in fact, you can use the same needle and thread as you do for sewing fabric. Cut a vinyl rectangle slightly larger than your photo, place the cutout on the quilt, and sew on three edges with a long machine stitch. Backtack for a few stitches at the top of each side edge for added reinforcement. Leave the top edge open so that you can slip in the photo. The photos are easy to remove when you want to wash the quilt or rotate the display.

SEWING TECHNIQUES

The projects in this book are made using standard quiltmaking and sewing techniques. Each project lists the fabrics, materials, and special tools required. The fabric amounts were calculated by tallying the measurements of the cut pieces and rounding up to the nearest ⅛ yard (0.1 m). Add on if you require a little more leeway. In addition to the items listed, you will need a sewing machine and iron, rotary cutting equipment, sewing shears, marking and measuring tools, and general sewing supplies.

Follow the project's cutting section to cut the fabric pieces to size. Dimensions for the cut pieces are listed wherever possible, with metric equivalents of the American measurements appearing in parentheses. Use strip cutting techniques to cut multiple pieces in the same size. For example, if a project calls for seven squares 5" x 5" (13 x 13 cm), cut a strip 5" (13 cm) wide across the width of the fabric and then subcut the strip into squares until you have the amount you need. Since metric conversions have been made for seam allowances and piece sizes, either system can be followed. Choose one system and follow it through to the completion of your quilt.

Follow the project's step-by-step assembly directions and illustrations to sew the fabric pieces together. Press each seam allowance in the direction indicated. Some quilters like to cut all their pieces at the beginning of the project and others like to alternate cutting and sewing. Either approach will work. Directions for specific sewing techniques follow.

Cutting Triangles

Two different triangles are used in this book: the half-square triangle and the quarter-square triangle. Both triangles have the same shape, but each type is cut by a different method, with a different grain direction (arrows) as the result. On a half-square triangle, the straight grain runs parallel to a short edge. On a quarter-square triangle, the straight grain runs parallel to the long edge.

Half-Square Triangle

Quarter-Square Triangle

Half-Square Triangles

Cut a square to the size indicated in the project directions. Cut the square diagonally in half, from corner to corner. This method is

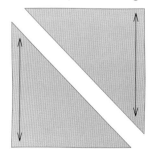

Cutting Half-Square Triangles

used to cut triangles for half-square triangle blocks and for the corners of quilts where the blocks are set on point.

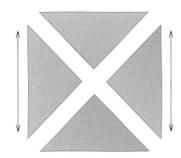

Cutting Quarter-Square Triangles

Quarter-Square Triangles

Cut a square to the size indicated in the project directions. Cut the square diagonally in half, from corner to corner. Don't move either piece. Line up the ruler on the opposite diagonal and cut again. This method is used to make setting triangles for blocks that are set on point.

Sew-and-Flip

The sew-and-flip method lets you create triangular patchwork shapes without actually cutting any triangles.

1. Cut two squares from contrasting fabrics to the size indicated in the project directions. Place the squares right sides together, with the lighter square on top. Draw a diagonal line on the lighter square, from corner to corner.

2. Stitch on the diagonal line.

3. Flip one triangle over so that the right side is visible. Press with an iron.

4. Trim out the bottom two layers ¼" (0.75 cm) from the stitching to remove the excess bulk.

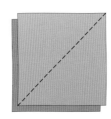

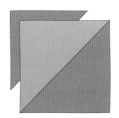

1. Draw   2. Stitch   3. Flip and Press   4. Trim

Pocket Appliqué

Pocket appliqué is a quick method for turning under a seam allowance and forming a smooth edge on appliqués. It works best on simple shapes, such as a heart. Cut a template of the shape from thin, stiff template plastic. You will also need a pencil.

1. Fold a piece of fabric in half, wrong side out (or place two pieces of the same fabric right sides together). Place the template on the wrong side. Trace around the template outline with a pencil.

2. Stitch on the marked line through both layers. Cut out the shape approximately ¼" (0.75 cm) beyond the stitching line. Clip cleavages to within a thread or two of the stitched line. Trim the seam allowance around a point to a little less than ¼" (0.75 cm).

3. Cut a small slit in the middle of one side, using small scissors or a sharp seam ripper. Be sure to slit through one layer of fabric only. Turn the shape right side out and poke out the corners and curves. Press well. Cut out the back layer ¼" (0.75 cm) from the seam, or leave as is for an appliqué that pops out from the background.

Tip: *Using the same fabric on both sides of the appliqué helps hide imperfections around the edges.*

4. Sew the appliqué to the background fabric. For an invisible look, whip by hand with matching thread. For a decorative look, thread a chenille needle with size 8 pearl cotton and work a blanket stitch or running stitch around the edge. Various machine stitches can also be used.

Using a Quilt Wall

When arranging blocks prior to sewing the quilt top, using a design wall is extremely helpful. A design wall is a large vertical surface that allows the quilter to arrange and rearrange blocks until a pleasing arrangement is achieved. With a vertical surface, in contrast to a horizontal surface such as the floor, all blocks are the same distance from your eye, allowing you to quickly see design "errors" such as too many blocks of one color in one row or in one corner of the quilt. A design wall allows the quilter to rearrange the blocks as desired

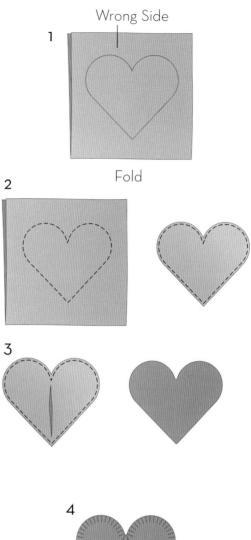

Wrong Side

1

Fold

2

3

4

Blanket Stitch

Running Stitch

without pinning and unpinning since the blocks "stick" to the surface. This allows for more playing and rearranging until the block arrangement pleases you.

I use a quilt wall, size 72" x 72" (183 cm x 183 cm) available from In The Beginning Fabrics, Seattle, Washington, for my design wall. It is a large, thick fleece surface that blocks stick to better than any other surface I have tried. I do not recommend using quilt batting because it will stretch. In a pinch, I have used cotton batting because it stretches much less than polyester. I do not recommend lighter weight surfaces such as flannel because the quilt blocks will need to be pinned to the flannel or they will fall off. Quilters do much more arranging and rearranging when the blocks can simply be pressed to the surface and stick with no pinning required.

I secure my quilt wall to the wall with push pins. For smaller holes, use regular straight pins placed 10" (25.5 cm) apart. When straight pins are removed and the wall taken down, pin holes will not be noticeable.

DISPLAY TIPS

There are various ways to display a quilt. The best way, from a longevity point of view, is to add a sleeve to the top back surface of the quilt and slide a board through the sleeve for hanging. The weight of the quilt is distributed along the entire length of the board, for less wear and tear on the quilt.

Hanging Sleeve

For a hanging sleeve, you'll need fabric, thread, a 1" x 2" (2.5 x 5.0 cm) wood board, two screw eyes, picture hanging wire, and a picture hanging hook. I prefer using a flat piece of wood rather than a dowel. The dowel rounds off and distorts the top of the quilt, whereas a board lies flat.

1. Cut a strip of fabric 6" (15.2 cm) wide x the length of the top edge of the quilt. You may have to piece two or more strips end to end to obtain the required length.

2. Fold in one end, wrong side in, by 1½" (3.8 cm). Press. Tuck the raw edge in to meet the fold line and press again, for a ¾" (1.9 cm) double fold. Stitch close to the second fold with matching thread.

3. Repeat step 2 at the opposite end.

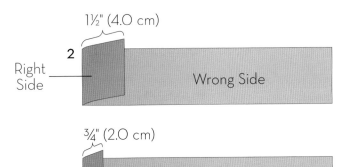

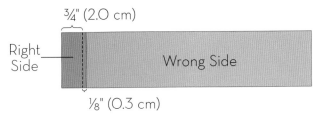

4. Fold the strip in half lengthwise, right side out. Stitch the long edges together. Refold so the seam is centered. Press.

Wrong Side — 4   Right Side

Seam Centered on Back Side —   Right Side

5. Center the quilt sleeve along the top back edge of the quilt, just below the binding. Whipstitch each folded edge to the quilt back with matching thread. Leave the ends open.

Tip: *You can also attach a sleeve when you bind the quilt. Follow steps 1–3 to make the sleeve. Fold it in half lengthwise, right side out. Align the raw edges with top back edge of the quilt. Stitch the binding in the usual way, catching the sleeve in the seam. After the binding is completed, whipstitch the bottom edge of the sleeve.*

6. Cut the wood board to a length 1" (2.5 cm) less than the quilt width. Insert the wood board through the sleeve. Attach a screw eye at each end. Attach picture hanging wire to the screw eyes, as you would for a picture frame. Hang on the wall from one or more picture hanging hooks.

Pinning

Pinning a quilt to the wall is another display option. For many years, I used pushpins, inserting them across the top of the quilt in the seam between the border and the binding. Using pushpins was easy; the drawback was that the thick shaft left holes in the quilt. Then I discovered short straight pins with a fairly thick shaft. These pins are much kinder to the quilt. They don't create holes and are less noticeable when you look at the quilt on the wall. I space them fairly close together so the quilt doesn't sag.

Using straight pins gives me flexibility. I can take down and put up quilts more quickly than I can when I use a sleeve, wood, wire, and a hook. When I remove a pinned quilt from the wall, I don't see pinholes in either the wall or the quilt. I can rotate my display, placing smaller quilts where larger ones once hung, without worrying about how to cover up the holes.

Foam Core Board

When a quilt is laden with memorabilia, I support it from the back with a foam core board. Foam core boards are available at framing shops, craft stores, and art galleries in sizes up to 40" x 60" (101.6 x 152.4 cm), and they can be cut to different sizes. There are two ways to use the board. One way is to create a large pocket on the back of the quilt (essentially, a second back with an opening at the top) and slip the board into it. Another way is to place the quilt on the board and insert pins from the front to hold it in place. Cut the foam core board slightly smaller than the quilt and turn the binding over the edges. This way, the board will not be visible from the front or sides when the quilt hangs on the wall. If the pins pierce clear through the board, bend down the points so that they don't stick anybody.

Taking Care of Quilts

The very best way to care for a quilt is to lay it flat on a bed, but if you have many quilts, that may not be an option for most of them. Here are some additional ideas:

• Fold your quilts in thirds to minimize the number of fold lines.

• Fold your quilts with the right side out.

• Refold your quilts every three or four months so the fold lines don't become "imbedded" in the quilt.

• Place acid-free tissue paper (available in a quilt or fabric shop or online), bunched up, inside the folds to keep fold lines from occurring.

• Place quilts you want to store in pillow cases or wrap them in clean sheets to protect them from dust but still allow them to breath.

• Never seal quilts in hard plastic containers or in plastic bags of any kind. Remember that cotton is a natural fiber and needs to breathe. If you don't allow your quilts to breathe, over time they will mold and mildew.

When necessary, wash your quilts using quilt soap and lay them flat to dry. In the winter, a clean utility table works well. Turn the quilt every day until it is completely dry. You can also use your dining room table, but cover it with clear plastic before you put your quilt on it.

Above all, enjoy your quilts. Remember, some quilts are made to be used. Not all quilts need to be "saved" to become heirlooms. If you love quilts, make them a part of your home, in every room of your house.

create

TROOP 239
CHELSEA Rachel
JULIA
GVIS
Lindsay
Kate Greta 1990-91

Remembering
When They Were Small

kelly alex

Look What I Drew
Quilt from a Child's Artwork

Are you reluctant to throw out all your kids' artwork? Quiltmaker Kathy Staley used photo transfers to save her boys' favorite pieces. She photocopied the paintings and drawings, shrinking some and enlarging others, and then made photo transfers onto white fabric. Each block in this picture gallery is "framed" with strips of colorful fabrics. The blocks are fitted together in a freestyle layout, with extra fabric strips, pieced blocks, and appliqués filling in the gaps. This is a truly creative approach, since everyone's artwork and quilt block composition will be different. In the quilt, you can find: a Log Cabin block, a patchwork star block, paintbox appliqués, a daisy appliqué, a checkerboard frame, and a signature block with fusible appliqués for names.

Featured Techniques

- quilting with children (page 7)
- photo transfer (page 8)
- freestyle block layout
- fusible appliqué
- embellishing with buttons
- pearl cotton embroidery

41½" x 57½" (105.5 x 146.5 cm). Made by Kathy Staley, Everett, Washington, 1998. Quilted by Becky Kraus.

Fabric

Note: Use fabrics that are at least 42" (106.5 cm) wide. Yardage may vary depending on the size of your artwork.

1 to 1½ yd. (0.9 to 1.4 m) white fabric for photo transfers

⅛ yd. (0.2 m) each of 18 assorted prints, to frame artwork

⅔ yd. (0.6 m) multicolored fabric for border

½ yd. (0.5 m) black solid for border and corner blocks

Scraps of assorted prints, plaids, solids

½ yd. (0.5 m) for binding

1⅔ yd. (1.5 m) backing

Materials

Eighteen pieces of children's original artwork

Photo transfer paper

Fusible web

46" x 62" batting (117 x 157.5 cm)

Buttons

Pearl cotton

Chenille needle

CUTTING

Assorted Prints

Cut 18 assorted strips, each 1¾" x 42" (4.5 x 106.5 cm) (A). Cut two strips of a single color if the perimeter of the artwork to be framed exceeds 36" (91.5 cm).

Multicolor

Cut five strips 3½" x 42" (9 x 106.5 cm). Piece together end to end to make one long strip (C).

Black Solid

Cut five strips 1½" x 42" (4 x 106.5 cm). Piece together end to end to make one long strip (B).
Cut four squares 3½" x 3½" (9 x 9 cm) (D).

ASSEMBLY

Note: Sew all pieces using a ¼" (0.75 cm) seam allowance.

1. Review the manufacturer instructions for your photo transfer paper. Enlarge or reduce each piece of artwork to the desired size. Make 18 photo transfers onto white fabric. Cut out each transfer ¼" (0.75 cm) beyond the image outline.

Tip: *Vary the sizes of the photo transfers to add interest and movement to your quilt design.*

2. Select an A strip to coordinate with each image. Cut two pieces from the A strip slightly longer than the side of the image. Sew the strips to the image. Press toward A (arrows). Cut off the excess strips even with the edges of the image. Repeat to sew two more strips to the top and bottom edges. Press. Trim. You will use up different amounts of each A strip, depending on the size of the image. If the image is large, you may need two A strips. Toss your extra pieces into your scrap pile for later use. Make 18 framed blocks.

3. Arrange the blocks as desired, using a quilt wall for arranging your photos and referring to the quilt photo (page 18) for placement ideas. Do not be concerned at this stage about holes in the design or how to facilitate the piecing. Strive for variety in the block sizes and good pattern and color contrast. Rearrange the pieces as needed to achieve a pleasing layout.

4. Design new blocks and strips to fill in the gaps in your layout. Search through your scraps to find compatible colors and patterns. Keep in mind that extra blocks and filler units don't have to be perfectly sized at the start. Have fun working out the design concept. You can trim the pieces for an exact fit later on.

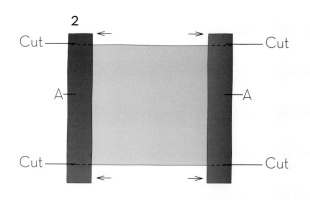

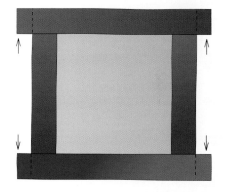

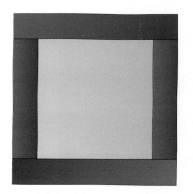

Make 18 Assorted

5. Sew the blocks and filler pieces together in small units. Press as desired. Join the small units together into rows or larger units as you are able. Trim as needed so that the edges align. Remember that you can also add more fabric as needed. The block section of the project quilt is 33" x 49" (84 x 124.5 cm), plus seam allowances, but your quilt size will probably be different.

6. Measure the quilt top vertically through the center. Cut two pieces this length from the B strip. Sew the pieces to the side edges of the quilt top. Press toward B. Measure the quilt top horizontally through the center. Cut two pieces this length from the B strip. Sew the pieces to the top and bottom edges of the quilt top. Press toward B.

Tip: *If your last border strip isn't long enough, piece in the additional length required.*

7. Measure the quilt top vertically through the center. Cut two pieces this length from the C strip for the side borders. Measure the quilt top horizontally through the center. Cut two pieces this length from the C strip. Sew a D square to each end of both strips. Press toward D for the top and bottom borders. Sew the borders to the side edges of the quilt top. Press toward C. Sew the borders to the top and bottom edges of the quilt top.

Tip: *Adjust the width of the inner and outer borders to suit your block layout. If you change the width of the outer border, be sure to adjust the size of the corner blocks to match.*

8. Trace four hearts (page 126) onto the paper side of the fusible web. Cut out each heart about ½" (1.5 cm) beyond the marked outline. Following the manufacturer's instructions, fuse each heart to the wrong side of a scrap fabric. Cut out on the marked outline. Fuse each heart to a black corner block.

9. Draw additional designs freehand onto fusible web. Ideas from the project quilt included long-stemmed flowers, a cloud with raindrops, and balloon-style letters that spell out the children's names. Fuse the web to the fabrics, cut out the appliqués, and fuse them to the quilt top.

Tip: *Draw letters for fusible appliqué in mirror image. The fusing process flips them back to the correct orientation.*

10. Layer the quilt top, batting, and backing. Quilt and bind as desired. Embellish the quilt top by sewing on buttons or embroidering designs with pearl cotton and a chenille needle.

Memories of Christmas Past
Displaying Ornaments Made by Your Children

When quiltmaker Lynn Ahlers made this charming holiday quilt for me, I knew just what to do with it! During their elementary school years, my children made a wide assortment of ornaments. Each year, we added new ones to our Christmas tree display, but with a tree so full, the special ornaments often got lost. This quilt lets me showcase each ornament inside its own Bow Tie block "wreath." It's quite a conversation starter. The quilt can also be hung vertically if that better fits your display space.

Featured Techniques

- sew-and-flip (page 12)
- Bow Tie blocks
- on-point blocks
- ornament display

48¾" x 64¼" (124 x 163.5 cm). Made by Lynn Ahlers, Issaquah, Washington, and Sandy Bonsib, Issaquah, Washington, 2003. Quilted by Becky Kraus.

Fabric

Note: Use fabrics that are at least 42" (106.5 cm) wide.

2¼ yd. (2.1 m) white print for blocks, border, and binding

⅞ yd. (0.8 m) off-white print for blocks and setting triangles

⅝ yd. (0.6 m) red print for blocks

⅝ yd. (0.6 m) dark green solid for blocks

½ yd. (0.5 m) red and green print for border

3 yd. (2.7 m) backing (vertical seam)

½ yd. (0.5 m) for binding

Materials

Fifteen handmade ornaments

CUTTING

White Print

Cut 54 squares 3¼" x 3¼" (8.5 x 8.5 cm) (A).

Cut two strips 3¼" x 31¼" (8.5 x 79.5 cm) (H).

Cut two strips 3¼" x 46¾" (8.5 x 119 cm), piecing as necessary (I).

Cut two strips 3½" x 42¾" (9 x 109 cm), piecing as necessary (L).

Cut two strips 3½" x 64¼" (9 x 163.5 cm), piecing as necessary (M).

Off-White Print

Cut 30 squares 3¼" x 3¼" (8.5 x 8.5 cm) (A).

Cut three squares 9½" x 9½" (24.5 x 24.5 cm). Cut diagonally in both directions to make 12 triangles (F).

Cut two squares 9½" x 9½" (24.5 x 24.5 cm). Cut diagonally in half to make four triangles (G).

Red Print

Cut 40 squares 1⅞" x 1⅞" (5 x 5 cm) (B).

Cut 40 squares 3¼" x 3¼" (8.5 x 8.5 cm) (C).

Dark Green Solid

Cut 44 squares 1⅞" x 1⅞" (5 x 5 cm) (D).

Cut 44 squares 3¼" x 3¼" (8.5 x 8.5 cm) (E).

Red and Green Print

Cut two strips 3¼" x 31¼" (8.5 x 79.5 cm) (J).

Cut two strips 3¼" x 46¾" (8.5 x 119 cm), piecing as necessary (K).

ASSEMBLY

Note: Sew all pieces using a ¼" (0.75 cm) seam allowance unless otherwise noted.

1. Sew-and-flip B to one corner of a white or off-white A. Press toward B. Make 40 units. Sew-and-flip D to each remaining A. Press toward D. Make 44 units.

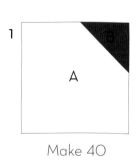

Make 40

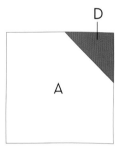

Make 44

2. Piece AB to C as shown. Press toward C (arrows). Make 40 ABC units.

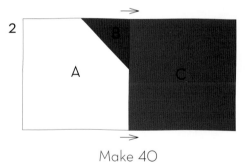

Make 40

3. Join two ABC units together as shown. Make 20 red Bow Tie blocks.

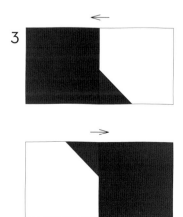

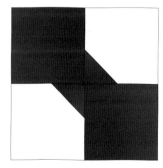

Bow Tie Block
Make 20

4. Repeat step 2 with the green pieces to make 44 ADE units. Press toward E. Join the ADE units together in pairs to make 22 green Bow Tie blocks.

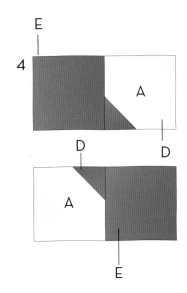

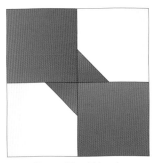

Bow Tie Block
Make 22

5. Arrange 20 red and 18 green Bow Tie blocks on point, alternating between red and green, as shown in the quilt photo (page 24) and quilt assembly diagram. Place the F setting triangles around the edges. Place the G triangles at the corners.

6. Stitch the blocks and setting triangles together in diagonal rows. Press the seams in opposite directions from row to row. Trim off any protruding triangle ears. Sew the rows together. Press in one direction. Add the corner triangles last. Press. Trim the quilt top to 31¼" x 46¾" (79.5 x 119 cm), centering the Bow Tie blocks, or about 2½" (6.5 cm) from the block points all around.

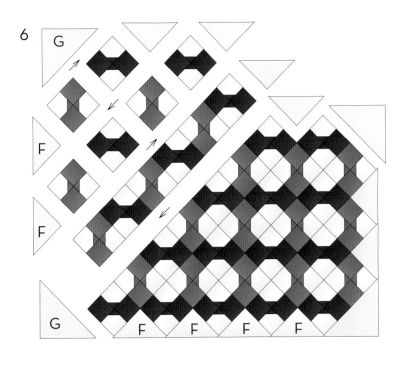

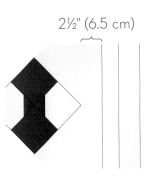

2½" (6.5 cm)

7. Sew H to J. Press toward J. Make 2. Sew I to K. Press toward K. Sew a green Bow Tie block to each end of IK. Make 2.

Make 2

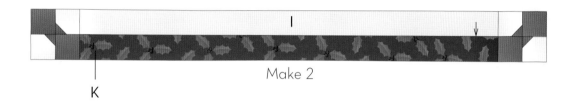

Make 2

8. Sew the HJ borders to the side edges of the quilt top, with H on the inside. Press toward HJ. Sew the IK borders to the top and bottom edges, with I on the inside. Press toward IK. Add L borders to the side edges. Press toward L. Add M borders to the top and bottom edges. Press toward M.

9. Layer the quilt top, batting, and backing. Quilt as desired. Bind with white print fabric.

10. Hang Christmas ornaments from ornament hooks. Insert the end of the hook (that would customarily be hung over a Christmas tree branch) into the quilt, piercing the top and batting. At the end of the holiday season, remove the ornaments and hooks before folding the quilt for storage.

TROOP 239
CHELSEA Rachel JULIA
Lindsay
Kate Greta 1990-91

I'll Never Forget Brownie Troop 239

A Group Project for Children

I used this project to introduce quilting to my daughter's Brownie troop. When you quilt with children, choose an easy-to-sew design. Keeping the project fun helps the children enjoy the process and achieve success while learning the basics. We traced designs on white blocks with permanent colored markers. Have an adult do the machine sewing if necessary. The quilt layers are tied, rather than quilted, which makes the finishing go faster. My daughter keeps this quilt carefully folded on a shelf in her closet. Whenever I look at it, I remember all the special times I shared with a wonderful group of girls.

Featured Techniques

- quilting with children (page 7)
- tracing on fabric
- signature block
- hand-tying

30 ½" x 30 ½" (77.5 x 77.5 cm). Made by Julia Ahlers, Kate Bickley, Greta Bloor, Lindsay Buckingham, Chelsea Carrigan, Rachel Zomick, and troop leader Sandy Bonsib, Issaquah, Washington, 1991. Hand-tied by Kate Bickley.

Fabric

Note: Use fabrics that are at least 42" (106.5 cm) wide.

1 yd. (0.9 m) dark blue novelty print

⅔ yd. (0.6 m) white

1 yd. (0.9 m) backing

Materials

Four designs from a coloring book

Permanent markers in colors that match the novelty print

Low-tack tape

Black fine-grit (#400) wet-dry sandpaper

35" x 35" (89 x 89 cm) batting

Embroidery floss or pearl cotton (size 8) for tying

Chenille needle, size 24

CUTTING

White
Cut five squares 10½" x 10½" (27 x 27 cm) (A).

Novelty Print
Cut four squares 10½" x 10½" (27 x 27 cm) (B).
Set aside the remaining novelty print for the binding.

ASSEMBLY

Note: Sew all pieces using a ¼" (0.75 cm) seam allowance.

1. Place a white A square on top of one design. Tape down the corners, if necessary, to prevent shifting. Trace the design with permanent colored markers. Make four different blocks.

2. Place the remaining white A square on sandpaper to prevent shifting during writing. Use permanent markers to write the troop number and date. Have each Brownie and the troop leader sign her name. Space the names casually and askew.

3. Lay out the A and B blocks in a Nine-Patch. Place the signature block in the center and the remaining A blocks in the corners.

4. Sew the blocks together in rows. Press toward B (arrows). Sew the rows together. Press.

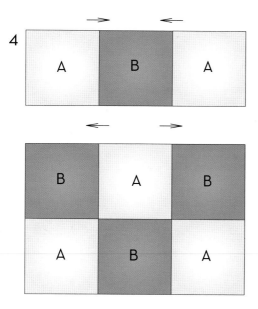

5. Layer the quilt top, batting, and backing. Thread a chenille needle with pearl cotton or embroidery floss. Tie the quilt at each block intersection and in the center of each block. Bind with dark blue novelty print.

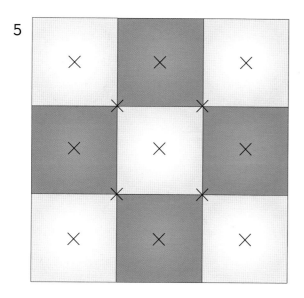

x = tie

When Kate Was One
A Quilt Featuring a Special Garment

When my children were young, I loved personalizing their clothing with their names and cute appliqués. The denim dress in this quilt was worn by my daughter Kate when she was one-and-a-half years old. One day, I took Kate and her brother Ben to the park and took their pictures as they were playing. Years later, when I was searching for items to embellish a childhood memory quilt, I discovered that I had both the dress and the pictures I took of Kate wearing it. To freshen up the dress after years of storage, I had it professionally laundered and ironed. Then I appliquéd it to the quilt top. I slipped the original photos into clear vinyl pockets sewn to the surface. Whimsical wire words, purchased from a craft store, add the final touch to this memory quilt for my now twenty-year-old little girl.

Featured Techniques

- clothing as appliqué
- clear vinyl pockets
- wire word embellishments

40½" x 40½" (103 x 103 cm). Made by Sandy Bonsib, Issaquah, Washington, 2003. Quilted by Kathy Staley.

Fabric

Note: Use fabrics that are at least 42" (106.5 cm) wide unless otherwise specified.

¾ yd. (0.7 m) muslin

⅝ yd. (0.6 m) medium red*

¼ yd. (0.3 m) light red*

⅛ yd. (0.2 m) dark red*

½ yd. (0.5 m) dark blue

½ yd. (0.5 m) total assorted medium and light blues

½ yd. (0.5 m) for binding

1¼ yd. (1.1 m) backing

*Use fabric 44" (112 cm) wide to avoid piecing long strips.

Materials

Child's garment, about 14" x 21" (35.5 x 53.5 cm)

Thread to match garment

Six 4" x 6" (10 x 15 cm) photographs

Six 5" x 7" (13 x 18 cm) clear vinyl rectangles

Low-tack tape

Six wire words

45" x 45" (114.5 x 114.5 cm) batting

CUTTING

Muslin
Cut one square 25" x 25" (63.5 x 63.5 cm).

Reds
Cut two medium red strips 9" x 44" (23 x 112 cm) (A).
Cut two light red strips 2" x 44" (5 x 112 cm) (B).
Cut one dark red strip 2" x 44" (5 x 112 cm) (C).

Blues
Cut five dark blue strips 2½" x 42" (6.5 x 106.5 cm) (D).
Cut five assorted medium and light blue strips 2½" x 42" (6.5 x 106.5 cm), piecing as needed (E).

Tip: Piece small assorted scraps together end to end to make a long strip of the desired length. You'll get a scrappy look along with the speed and convenience of strip piecing.

ASSEMBLY

Note: Sew all pieces using a ¼" (0.75 cm) seam allowance.

1. Arrange the five red strips in the following order: A B C B A. Sew the long edges together to make a 22" x 44" (56 x 112 cm) strip set. Press each seam toward the darker fabric (arrows).

2. Cut the strip set in half, to make two 22" x 22" (57.5 x 57.5 cm) squares. Cut each square diagonally in half to make four large triangles.

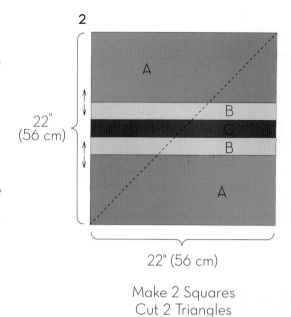

2

22" (56 cm)

A
B
C
B
A

22" (56 cm)

Make 2 Squares
Cut 2 Triangles

3. Mark the midpoint of the long edge of each triangle. Mark the midpoint of each edge of the muslin square. Sew two triangles to opposite edges of the square, right sides together and midpoints matching. Press toward the triangles. Trim as shown.

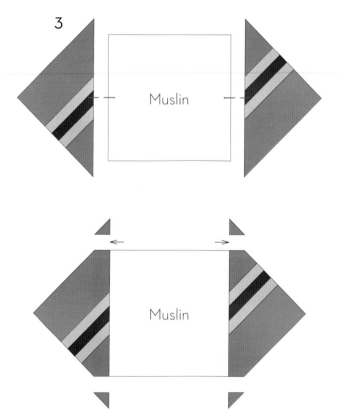

3

Muslin

Muslin

4. Sew two triangles to the remaining edges of the muslin square. Press. Trim to 36½" x 36½" (93 x 93 cm), centering the muslin square on-point.

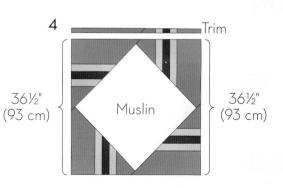

4

Trim

36½" (93 cm)

Muslin

36½" (93 cm)

5. Sew D to E. Press toward D. Make five DE strip sets. Cut into segments 4½" (11.5 cm) wide. Make 40 assorted DE units.

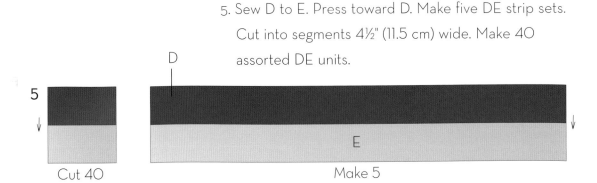

5

Cut 40

D

E

Make 5

6. Arrange nine DE units along each side edge of the large patchwork unit. Place 11 DE units along the top and bottom edges. Alternate the darker blue rectangles, as shown in the quilt photo (page 34), for an elongated checkerboard look. Once you have an arrangement you like, sew the DE units together to make four pieced border strips. Press as desired. Sew the border strips to the sides of the quilt top, then the top and bottom of the quilt top, pressing after each addition.

7. Layer the quilt top, batting, and backing. Quilt and bind as desired.

8. Center the child's garment on the muslin diamond. Tack in place with matching thread, taking as many stitches as needed to attach the garment securely.

9. Arrange the photos around the garment, collage-style. Place a clear vinyl rectangle over each photo. Tape the vinyl in place (do not pin), and then remove the photo. Set the machine for a long stitch length. Stitch around three sides of each vinyl piece, backtacking near the top edge for added reinforcement. Leave the top edge open. Slip each photo into its pocket. Hand-sew a wire word to the quilt above or below each photo.

Tip: Set the photo pockets at an angle for a jaunty look. The pockets can overlap slightly—just be sure to allow enough room to insert the photos.

SEWING SUSA
50 GOLD EYE NEEDLE
WITH THREADER

Remembering

Everyday Life

44

MECHE

55

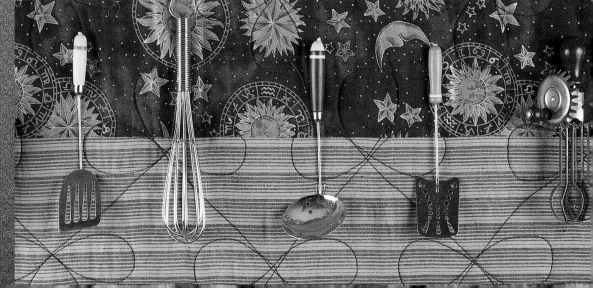

A Team to Remember
Celebrating a Favorite Sports Team

This sports theme quilt features my son's eight most favorite player names and numbers, all cut from purchased T-shirts. The logos on the smaller blocks were cut from the T-shirt sleeves, and another T-shirt was the source for the team name and logo in the center block. Fusible knit interfacing, applied across the grain, helps stabilize the stretchy knit fabric.

Featured Techniques

• T-shirt blocks

70½" x 70½" (179.5 x 179.5 cm). Made by Sandy Bonsib, Issaquah, Washington, 2003. Quilted by Becky Kraus.

Fabric

Note: Use fabrics that are at least 42" (106.5 cm) wide.

2¼ yd. (2.1 m) team color for sashing, borders, and binding

½ yd. (0.5 m) white for center diamond

¼ yd. (0.3 m) player T-shirt color

4½ yd. (4.1 m) backing

Materials

Extra-large T-shirt with team name and logo

Eight extra-large individual player T-shirts

5⅝ yd. (5.1 m) fusible knit interfacing, 22" (56 cm) wide

76" x 76" (193 x 193 cm) batting

CUTTING

Team Color

Cut eight rectangles 6" x 17" (15.5 x 43.5 cm) (C).

Cut eight rectangles 6" x 9" (15.5 x 23 cm) (B).

Cut four strips 6" x 61" (15.5 x 155.5 cm), piecing as needed (D).

White

Cut four rectangles 6" x 11½" (15.5 x 29.5 cm) (A).

T-Shirt Color

See the tip under step 2.

T-Shirts

Cut each T-shirt apart as shown. Take care not to damage the player names or logos.

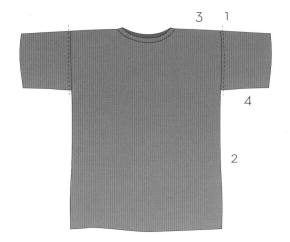

1. Cut off sleeves
2. Cut side seams
3. Cut shoulder seams
4. Cut underarm seams

Fusible Knit Interfacing

Cut nine squares about 20" x 20" (51 x 51 cm).

Cut eight squares about 7" x 7" (18 x 18 cm).

ASSEMBLY

Note: Sew all pieces using a ¼" (0.75 cm) seam allowance.

1. Lay the T-shirt piece with the large team logo face-down on a padded surface. Fuse a 20" x 20" (51 x 51 cm) square of knit interfacing to the wrong side, following the manufacturer's instructions. In the same way, fuse a large square of knit interfacing to the wrong side of each player's name and number.

Tip: *Knits have a less stretchy grain and a more stretchy grain. Place the stretchier grain of the fusible interfacing perpendicular to the stretchier grain of the T-shirt fabric. When the two pieces are fused together, they will stabilize one another for a suprisingly unstretchy square.*

2. Trim the fused pieces made in step 1 to 17" x 17" (43.5 x 43.5 cm), centering the lettering and numbers.

Tip: *If a fused piece is too small to trim to 17" x 17" (43.5 x 43.5 cm) (because of an interfering neckline, for example), you can extend it and add a border at the same time. Trim the edges evenly, to square up the block. Cut four strips, each 18" (46 cm) long and of a generous width, from fabric that is the same color as the player T-shirts. Sew a strip to each edge, pressing after each addition. Then trim the entire piece to 17" x 17" (43.5 x 43.5 cm), centering the logo. Be sure to cut the border strips wider than you think will be necessary. Use this method to make the team logo block.*

3. Fuse a 7" x 7" (18 x 18 cm) square of knit interfacing to the wrong side of a small logo from a T-shirt sleeve. Make eight total. Trim each piece to 6" x 6" (15.5 cm), centering the logo.

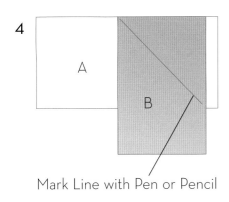

4

Mark Line with Pen or Pencil

4. Place B on A, right sides together and at a right angle, as shown. Allow about ¼" (0.75 cm) of A to extend at the right. Use a pencil and ruler to mark a diagonal line on the wrong side of B. The extension will help you align the ruler accurately.

5. Move B ¼" (0.75 cm) to the right until the edges are aligned. Machine-stitch on the marked line. Trim ¼" (0.75 cm) beyond the stitching line. Press toward B (arrow).

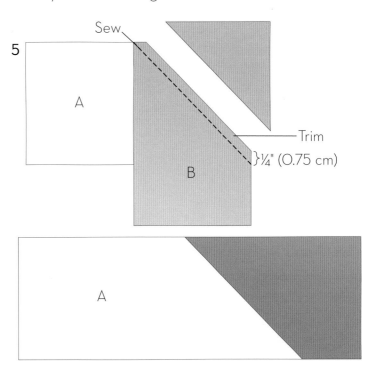

5

Sew

A

Trim

}¼" (0.75 cm)

B

A

6

B   A   B

Make 4

6. Repeat steps 4 and 5 to stitch another B to the opposite end of A. Trim equal amounts from both ends, as needed, to make a 6" x 17" (15.5 x 43.5 cm) unit. Make four AB units.

7. Arrange the T-shirt blocks, AB units, and C sashing strips as shown in the quilt photo (page 40) and quilt assembly diagram. The AB units will form a white diamond around the team logo block at the center.

8. Sew the pieces together in rows. Press toward AB or C. Sew the rows together. Press.

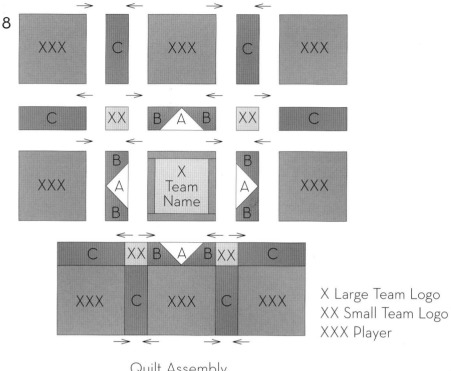

Quilt Assembly

X Large Team Logo
XX Small Team Logo
XXX Player

9. Sew a D border to each side edge of the quilt top. Press toward D. Stitch a small logo block to both ends of each remaining D. Press toward D. Add the borders to the top and bottom edges of the quilt. Press.

Tip: *Fold each border strip in half to find the midpoint and mark with a pin. Do the same for each edge of the quilt. Match up the ends and the midpoints when you pin the borders to the quilt for a more accurate fit.*

10. Layer the quilt top, batting, and backing. Quilt and bind as desired.

Tip: *Just for fun, buy a small stuffed toy of the team mascot. Make a special pocket on the quilt and slip the mascot inside.*

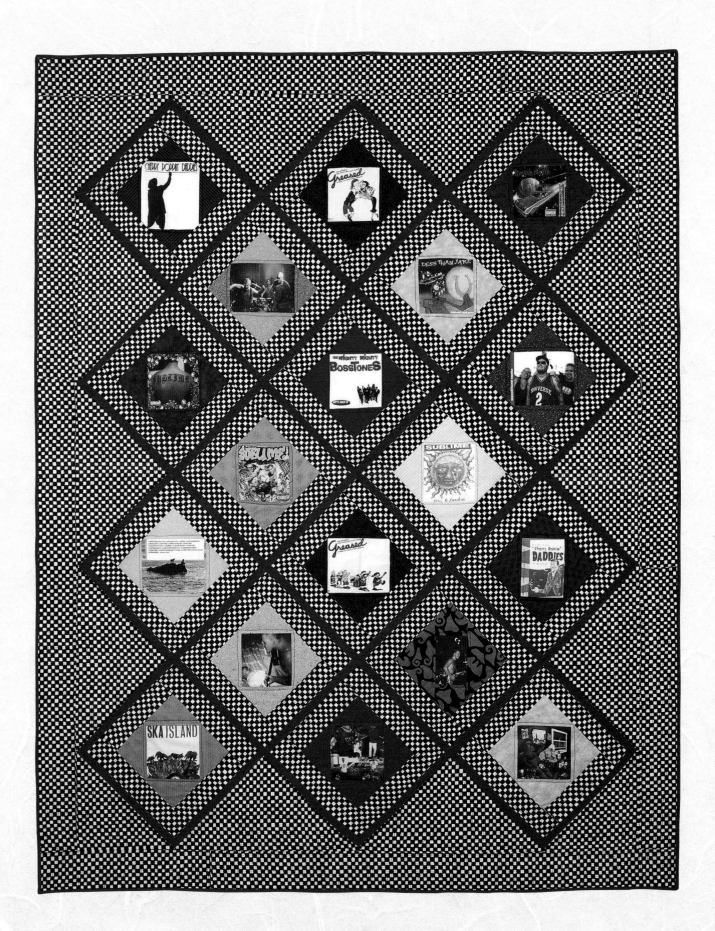

Play That Song Again

A Memory Quilt Featuring CD or Album Covers

When Lynn Ahler's daughter, Julia, went to college on the East Coast, Lynn wanted to make her a quilt to remind her of things she had always enjoyed back home. Julia is a devoted fan of certain music groups and frequently attends their concerts. She chose eighteen CD covers, which Lynn then copied onto fabric using a photo transfer technique. The photo transfer blocks are displayed against a black-and-white print accented with red sashing and binding. The result is a clean, graphic look. For a fan of the music of another time, try the same idea with old record album covers.

Featured Techniques

- photo transfer (page 8)
- on-point blocks

58½" x 75½" (149 x 192 cm). Made by Lynn Ahlers, Issaquah, Washington, 2003. Quilted by Becky Kraus.

Fabric

Note: Use fabrics that are at least 42" (106.5 cm) wide. Choose colors that coordinate with the CD covers.

⅝ yd. (0.6 m) white for photo transfers

¼ yd. (0.3 m) each of 18 assorted prints and solids, or 18 pieces at least 5" x 10" (13 x 25.5 cm) each

3½ yd. (3.2 m) black-and-white check

¾ yd. (0.7 m) red

3¾ yd. (3.4 m) backing

Materials

Eighteen CD covers

Photo transfer paper

63" x 80" (160 x 203 cm) batting

CUTTING

Assorted Prints and Solids

Cut two squares 5" x 5" (13 x 13 cm) from each fabric, or 36 squares total. Cut diagonally in half to make 72 triangles (A).

Black-and-White Check

Cut 36 strips 2¼" x 8" (6 x 20.5 cm) (B).

Cut 36 strips 2¼" x 11½ (6 x 29 cm) (C).

Cut three squares 19" x 19" (48.5 x 48.5 cm). Cut diagonally in both directions to make 12 triangles (You will use ten.) (I).

Cut two squares 11" x 11" (28x 28 cm). Cut diagonally in half to make four triangles (J).

Cut two strips 4¼" x 68" (11 x 173 cm), piecing as needed (K).

Cut two strips 4¼" x 60½" (11 x 154 cm), piecing as needed (L).

Red

Cut 24 strips 1¼" x 11½" (3.5 x 29.5 cm) (D).

Cut two strips 1¼" x 13" (3.5 x 33.5 cm) (E).

Cut two strips 1¼" x 36½" (3.5 x 93 cm) (F).

Cut two strips 1¼" x 60" (3.5 x 152.5 cm), piecing as needed (G).

Cut one strip 1¼" x 71" (3.5 x 180.5 cm), piecing as needed (H).

ASSEMBLY

Note: Sew all pieces using a ¼" (0.75 cm) seam allowance.

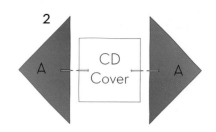

1. Review the manufacturer instructions for your photo transfer paper. Copy the CD covers, without enlarging or reducing, and make 18 photo transfers onto muslin. Cut out each transfer ¼" (0.75 cm) beyond the image outline.

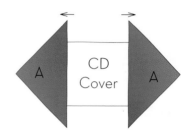

Tip: This quilt design and layout can be adjusted according to the number of covers you wish to display.

2. Choose four matching A triangles to coordinate with one image. Mark the midpoint of the long edge of each triangle. Mark the midpoint of each edge of the image. Sew two A triangles to the side edges of the image, right sides together and midpoints matching. Press toward A (arrows). Sew the remaining two triangles to the top and bottom edges in the same way. Press. Trim to 8" x 8" (20.5 x 20.5 cm), centering the image. Make 18 blocks.

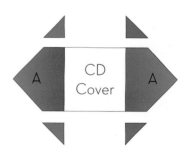

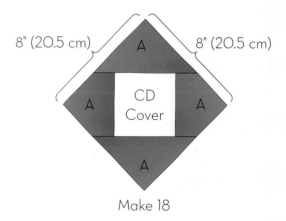

Make 18

3. Sew two B strips to opposite edges of each block. Press toward B. Sew two C strips to the remaining edges. Press toward C.

3

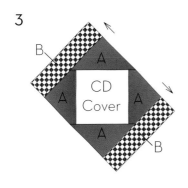 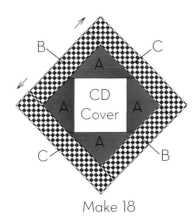 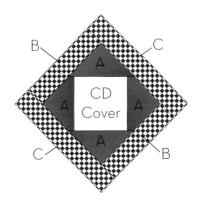

Make 18

4. Arrange the blocks on point, inserting D sashing strips in between and at the ends, as shown in the block layout diagram. Sew the blocks and sashing together in diagonal rows. Press toward D.

4

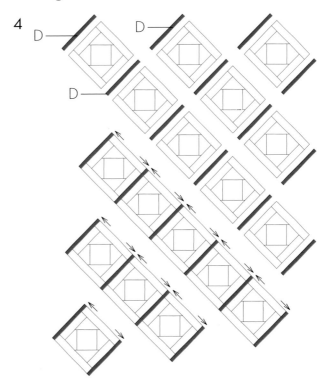

5. Place the remaining sashing strips and the setting triangles in the layout, as shown in the quilt assembly diagram. Sew the E, F, and G sashing strips to the block rows. Press toward the sashing. Join the I triangles. Press toward I. Trim off the triangle ears. Add sashing H. Press toward H. Join the rows together. Press. Add the corner triangles. Press.

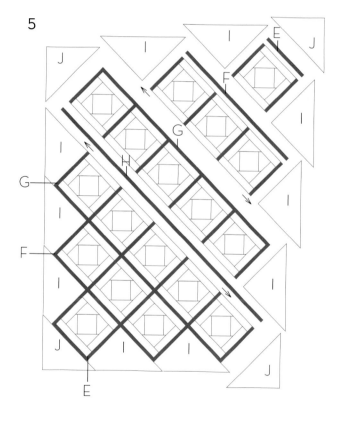

6. Trim the quilt top to 51" x 68" (130 x 173 cm), or about ½" (0.75 cm) beyond the block points all around.

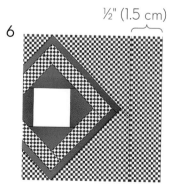

7. Sew the K borders to the sides of the quilt top. Press toward K. Sew the L borders to the top and bottom edges. Press toward L.

8. Layer the quilt top, batting, and backing. Quilt as desired. Bind with red fabric.

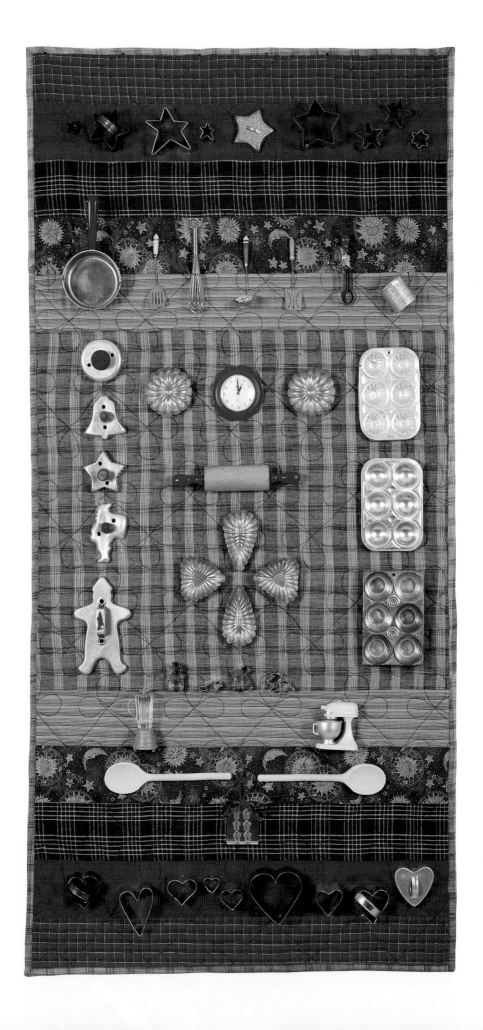

Grandma's Kitchen
Displaying Memorabilia

This warm, homey quilt provides a backdrop for a collection of small, vintage kitchen utensils, including some from children's play sets. Most of the collection is owned by Sue Van Gerpen. When I was working on the quilt, I found a few more pieces to add. Even though the embellishments are small, their weight adds up. To keep the quilt from stretching, mount it on a foam core board (page 15) or add a large pocket to the back of the quilt and slip the foam core into it.

Featured Techniques

- glued-on embellishments

- foam core board support (page 15)

27½" x 57½" (70 x 146.5 cm). Made by Sandy Bonsib, Issaquah, Washington, 2003. Quilted by Becky Kraus.

Fabric

Note: Use fabrics that are at least 42" (106.5 cm) wide.

1 yd. (0.9 m) gray plaid for center square and binding

¼ yd. (0.3 m) gold stripe

¼ yd. (0.3 m) blue novelty print

¼ yd. (0.3 m) black plaid

¼ yd. (0.3 m) red-and-green plaid

¼ yd. (0.3 m) red plaid

2 yd. (1.8 m) backing fabric

Materials

32" x 62" (81.5 x 157.5 cm) batting

Assorted antique kitchen utensils

Toy kitchen utensils

Hot-glue gun

Needle

Strong thread

27" x 57" (68.5 x 145 cm) foam core board

Short straight pins

CUTTING

Gray Plaid

Cut one rectangle 22½" x 27½" (57.5 x 70 cm) (A).

Set aside the remaining gray plaid for the binding.

Accent Fabrics

Cut two strips 4" x 27½" (10.5 x 70 cm) from each fabric, or ten strips total. Label as follows:

gold stripe (B)

blue novelty print (C)

black plaid (D)

red-and-green plaid (E)

red plaid (F).

ASSEMBLY

Note: Sew all pieces using a ¼" (0.75 cm) seam allowance.

1. Arrange pieces A, B, C, D, E, and F as shown. Sew the pieces together. Press as desired.

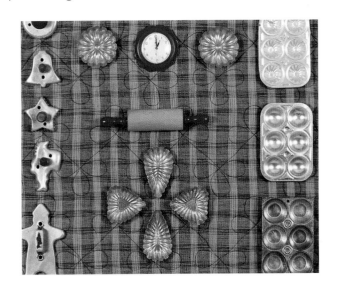

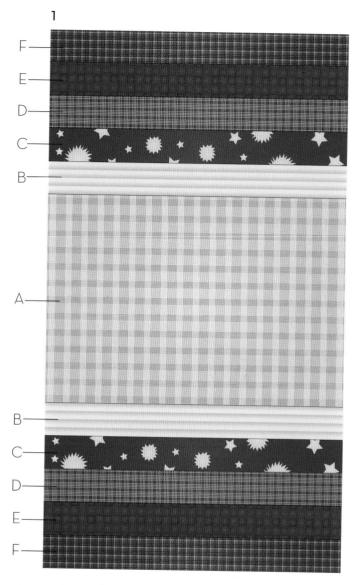

2. Layer the quilt top, batting, and backing. Quilt as
   desired. Bind with gray plaid.

3. Arrange your collection of kitchen memorabilia on the
   quilt surface. Cluster similar items horizontally, vertically,
   or in groups, as shown in the quilt photo (page 52).
   Attach the pieces using a hot-glue gun or a needle and
   strong thread.

4. Mount the finished quilt on foam core board and secure
   with straight pins for added support.

Great Grandmother's Sewing Notions
Theme Quilt with Family Heirlooms

Sue Van Gerpen made this quilt to display sewing cards and other needlework memorabilia that once belonged to her great grandmother, Anna Sommers. When Anna died, her sewing supplies were given to Sue. The quilt hangs in Sue's sewing room, where it provides lively decor as well as a link to her family's past.

Techniques to Try

- glued-on embellishments

- foam core board support (page 15)

24½" x 39" (62.5 x 99.5 cm). Made and quilted by Sue Van Gerpen, North Bend, Washington, 2002.

Fabric

Note: Use fabrics that are at least 42" (106.5 cm) wide.

½ to ¾ yd. (0.5 to 0.7 m) muslin for photo transfers

1½ yd. (1.4 m) medium floral for sashing, borders, bias strip, and binding

1½ yd. (1.4 m) light floral for piecing and corner blocks

⅓ yd. (0.3 m) stripe for triangles

⅛ yd. (0.2 m) red print

⅛ yd. (0.2 m) green print

Scraps of coordinating red and green prints

1 to 1¼ yd. (0.9 to 1.2 m) backing

Materials

Seven assorted vintage sewing cards

Photo transfer paper

29" x 43" (74 x 109 cm) batting

Wooden darning egg

Buttons (on cards and loose)

"Sewing Susan" paper needle packet

Handmade needle case

Other sewing memorabilia

Glue gun

CUTTING

Medium Floral
Cut one strip 2" x 19" (5.5 x 48.5 cm) (F).
Cut two strips 3¼" x 33½" (8.5 x 85.5 cm) (H).
Cut two strips 3¼" x 19" (8.5 x 48.5 cm) (I).
Cut four bias strips 1⅛" x 18" (3 x 46 cm) (K).
Set aside the remaining medium floral for the binding.

Light Floral
Cut one rectangle 13½" x 19" (34.5 x 48.5 cm) (G).
Cut four squares 3¼" x 3¼" (8.5 x 8.5 cm) (J).

Stripe
Cut two squares 10½" x 10½" (27 x 27 cm). Cut diagonally in half to make four triangles. You will use the four triangles with stripes running parallel to the long edge (E).

Red Print
Cut two strips 1" x 11½" (3 x 29 cm) (A).
Cut two strips 1" x 12½" (3 x 32 cm) (B).

Green Print
Cut two strips 1½" x 12½" (3 x 32 cm) (C).
Cut two strips 1½" x 14" (3 x 35.5 cm) (D).

ASSEMBLY

Note: Sew all pieces using a ¼" (0.75 cm) seam allowance except where noted.

1. Review the manufacturer instructions for your photo transfer paper. Enlarge one sewing card image to about 6" x 8" (15 x 20.5 cm) and make a photo transfer onto muslin. Use a ruler and pencil to draw an 11½" x 11½" (29 x 29 cm) square on point around the image, centering the image inside. Cut out the muslin square on the marked outline. Make photo transfers of the remaining images at their actual size. Cut out each transfer ¼" (0.75 cm) beyond the image outline.

2. Sew two red A strips to opposite edges of the muslin square. Press toward A. Sew two red B strips to the remaining two edges of the muslin square. Press toward B. Repeat to add two green C strips and two green D strips, pressing after each addition.

3. Mark the midpoint of the long edge of each triangle E. Mark the midpoint of each edge of the muslin unit. Sew two E triangles to opposite edges of the muslin unit, right sides together and midpoints matching. Press toward E (arrows). Trim the ears. Repeat to add the two remaining E triangles. Press. Trim to 19" x 19" (48.5 x 48.5 cm).

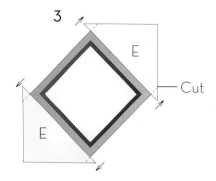

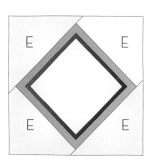

Trim to 19" x 19"
(48.5 cm x 48.5 cm)
Make 1

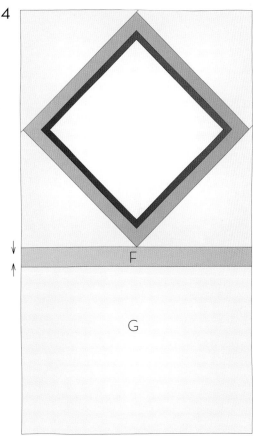

4

F

G

4. Arrange the block, F, and G as shown. Sew F to the block. Press toward F. Sew G to F. Press toward F.

5. Sew the H borders to the side edges of the quilt top. Press toward H. Sew a J square to each end of I. Press toward J. Make two. Sew the IJ borders to the top and bottom edges of the quilt top. Press toward IJ.

6. Piece the K bias strips together end to end. Press seams open. Fold the strip in half lengthwise, wrong side in, and stitch the long edges together in a ⅛" (0.3 cm) seam. Press strip flat, with seam centered on back. Arrange the bias strip on the muslin, looping it around the photo transfer image, as shown in the quilt photo (page 56). Appliqué by hand with matching thread.

Right Side

6

Wrong Side

K

⅛" (0.3 cm) Seam

7. Cut strips 1" to 1¼" (2.5 to 3 cm) wide from the red and green scraps. Repeat the step 2 technique to add red and green borders around the remaining photo transfers from step 1. Or place an image on a contrasting rectangle and appliqué a contrasting bias strip around it. Arrange the photo transfers on the quilt top, overlapping them collage-style, as shown in the quilt photo (page 56). Fold in the raw edges ¼" (0.75 cm) and appliqué by hand or machine.

8. Layer the quilt top, batting, and backing. Quilt and
   bind as desired.

9. Arrange the sewing memorabilia on the quilt surface.
   Tack in place with needle and thread. Use a glue gun
   to affix heavier items, such as a darning egg.

Tip: *Fold four small squares of fabric into triangles and
tuck in the raw edges. Stitch the triangles to the surface
as mounting corners for a paper needle packet.*

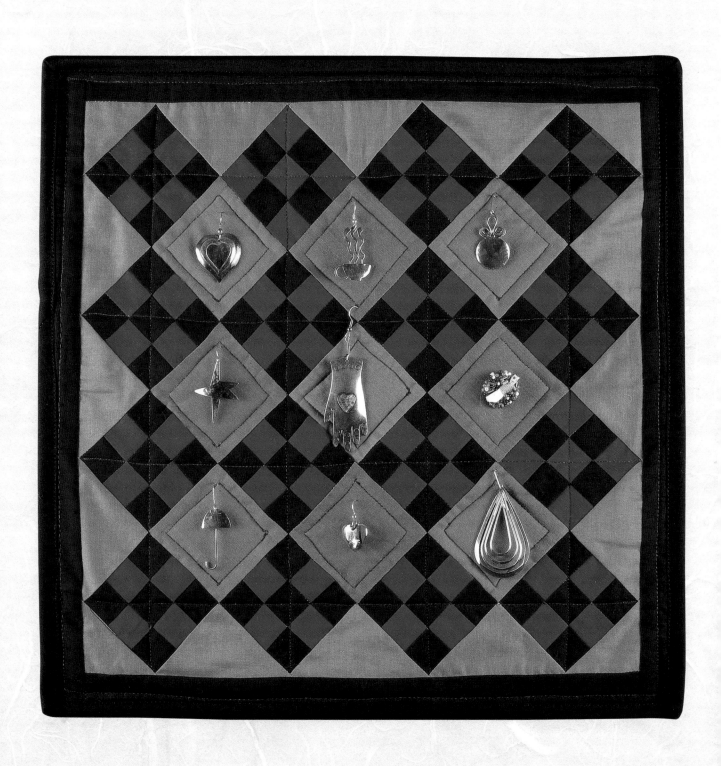

Jewelry with a Past

A Quilt to Display Old Earrings, Charms, or Other Jewelry

Women choose their earrings carefully. When part of a set gets lost, or an outfit is no longer in style, what happens to those favorite pieces? This Amish-style quilt features the "one left" of what used to be my favorite pairs of earrings. There's a heart in a hand, a triple heart, an úmbrella (I do live outside of rainy Seattle, after all), and a coffee cup. To attach drop earrings, simply hook the earring wires into the fabric. Small pins or charms can also be attached. If the jewelry is precious or valuable, you may wish to frame the quilt under glass.

Featured Techniques

- Nine-Patch block
- on-point blocks
- embellishing with jewelry

15½" x 15½" (39.5 x 39.5 cm). Made by Sandy Bonsib, Issaquah, Washington, 2003. Quilted by Becky Kraus.

Fabric

Note: Use fabrics that are at least 42" (106.5 cm) wide.

⅜ yd. (0.4 m) black for Nine-Patch blocks, borders, and binding

¼ yd. (0.3 m) blue-violet

¼ yd. (0.3 m) blue for Nine-Patch blocks

⅛ yd. (0.2 m) violet

⅛ yd. (0.2 m) red-violet

½ yd. (0.5 m) for backing

Materials

20" x 20" (51 x 51 cm) batting

Nine single earrings

CUTTING

Black

Cut three strips 1¼" x 42" (3.5 x 106.5 cm) (A).
Cut two strips 1¼" x 14" (3.5 x 36 cm) (H).
Cut two strips 1¼" x 15½" (3.5 x 39.5 cm) (I).
Set aside the remaining black for the binding.

Blue-Violet

Cut three squares 4½" x 4½" (11.5 x 11.5 cm). Cut diagonally in both directions to make 12 triangles (F).
Cut two squares 3" x 3" (8 x 8 cm). Cut diagonally in half to make four triangles (G).
Cut one square 2¾" x 2¾" (7.5 x 7.5 cm) (C).

Blue

Cut three strips 1¼" x 42" (3.5 x 106.5 cm) (B).

Violet

Cut four squares 2¾" x 2¾" (7.5 x 7.5 cm) (D).

Red-Violet

Cut four squares 2¾" x 2¾" (7.5 x 7.5 cm) (E).

ASSEMBLY

Note: Sew all pieces using a ¼" (0.75 cm) seam allowance.

1. Sew two A strips to one B strip as shown. Press toward A. Cut the ABA strip set into 30 segments 1¼" (3.5 cm) wide.

Cut 30 Segments

2. Sew two B strips to one A strip as shown. Press toward
   A. Cut the BAB strip set into 18 segments 1¼" (3.5 cm)
   wide.

Cut 18 Segments

3. Arrange the segments in groups of three to make 16
   Nine-Patch blocks, as shown. Note that there are two
   "renegade" blocks. Sew the segments together. Press.

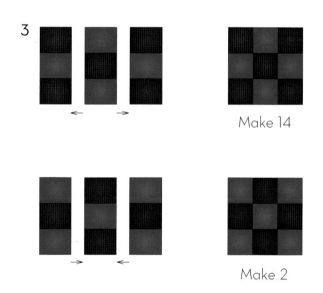

Make 14

Make 2

4. Arrange the Nine-Patch blocks and plain blocks C, D,
   and E on point, as shown in the color photo (page 62)
   and the quilt assembly diagram. Note the placement of
   the two renegade blocks. Place F setting triangles
   around the edges. Place G triangles at the corners.

Other Themes

Prom jewelry

Bracelet charms

Grandmother's costume
jewelry

Souvenir pins purchased
on trips

5. Sew the blocks and setting triangles together in diagonal rows. Press toward the plain blocks and the triangles. Join the rows, pressing all the seams in one direction. Add the corner triangles last. Press.

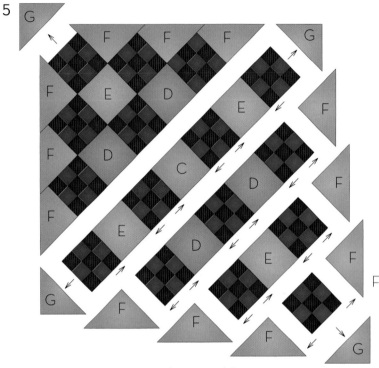

Quilt Assembly

6. Trim the quilt top to 14" x 14" (36 cm x 36 cm), or about ¼" (0.75 cm) from the block points all around.

7. Sew the H borders to the side edges of the quilt top. Press toward H. Sew the I borders to the top and bottom edges. Press toward I.

8. Layer the quilt top, batting, and backing. Quilt as desired. Bind with black fabric.

9. Hand-sew or attach nine single earrings to the quilt top so that they dangle in front of each solid block when the quilt is hung.

¼" (0.75 cm)

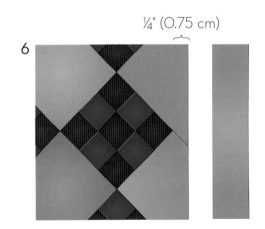

Love,
Paige Magley

y 80TH AND WISHING
NY MORE! THANKS
NG A GREAT FATHER-
AND "GRAMPY"
CHILDREN

Remembering Milestones

I REMEMBER:
Mom and Dad might not
always be right, but most of
the time they are! Love,
Julie

Now, as always, the most
automated appliance in a
household is the mother.
Beverly Jones

It's a Boy!

Quilt with Best Wishes from Friends and Family

When Sue Van Gerpen announced that she would soon become a mom after many years of waiting, her close friends gave her a baby shower. One of the shower activities was to have each guest write a short message and sign a signature block for this quilt. These handwritten messages were arranged into four heart shapes on the surface of the quilt—a continuing reminder to Sue of her friends' love and support.

Featured Techniques

- group quilt
- signature blocks
- sew-and-flip (page 12)

48" x 57½" (122 x 146.5 cm). Made by Sue Van Gerpen, North Bend, Washington, and Sandy Bonsib, Issaquah, Washington, with help from Sherry Laatsch, North Bend, Washington, 2003. Quilted by Becky Kraus.

Fabric

Note: Use fabrics that are at least 42" (106.5 cm) wide.

⅛ yd. (0.2 m) each of 29 assorted medium and dark blues

¾ yd. (0.7 m) muslin for signature blocks

½ yd. (0.5 m) dark blue for border

½ yd. (0.5 m) for binding

3⅝ yd. (3.3 m) backing

Materials

Permanent fine-point pens (.5mm or .8mm)

Black fine-grit (#400) wet-dry sandpaper

52" x 62" (132 x 157.5 cm) batting

CUTTING

Assorted Blues
Cut 64 squares 3⅝" x 3⅝" (9.5 x 9.5 cm) (A).
Cut 24 strips 2⅞" x 42" (7.5 x 106.5 cm) (B).

Muslin
Cut 32 squares 5¼" x 5¼" (13.5 x 13.5 cm) (C).

Dark Blue
Cut two strips 2⅞" x 43¼" (7.5 x 110 cm), piecing as needed (D).
Cut two strips 2⅞" x 57½" (7.5 x 146.5 cm), piecing as needed (E).

ASSEMBLY

Note: Sew all pieces using a ¼" (0.75 cm) seam allowance.

1. Sew-and-flip two A squares to diagonally opposite corners of muslin C. Press toward A (arrows). Make 32 blocks total.

2. Have friends and family sign their names and write messages on the muslin portion of the blocks with a permanent fine-point pen. Place the blocks on sandpaper to prevent shifting.

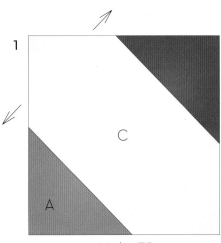

Make 32

3. Choose any two contrasting B strips. Sew the strips together along one long edge. Press toward the darker fabric. Make 12 strip sets. Cut into 134 segments 2⅞" (7.5 cm) wide.

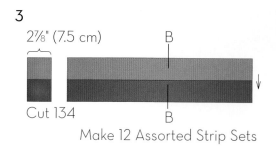

3

2⅞" (7.5 cm)

B

Cut 134

B

Make 12 Assorted Strip Sets

4. Arrange two different segments in a Four-Patch, with the darker squares diagonally opposite, as shown. Sew together. Press as desired. Make 67 assorted Four-Patch blocks.

4

Make 67

5. Arrange the signature blocks and Four-Patch blocks as shown in the quilt photo (page 68) and quilt assembly diagram. Rotate the signature blocks to form four large hearts. Make sure none of the writing on the signature blocks is upside down.

6. Sew the blocks together in rows. Press the seams in opposite directions from row to row. Sew the rows together. Press.

7. Sew the D borders to the top and bottom edges of the quilt top. Press toward D. Sew the E borders to the side edges of the quilt top. Press toward E.

8. Layer the quilt top, batting, and backing. Quilt and bind as desired.

5

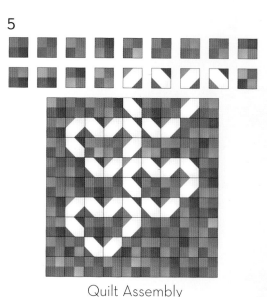

Quilt Assembly

Graduation Day

Celebrate with a Quilt Made from the Gown and Other Mementoes

My son's high school graduation gown provided the rich purple fabric for this memorabilia collage. I added gold satin to the palette so both school colors are represented. A graduation photo, cap and tassel, and recognition pins complete the picture. The piecing is easy, and the finished quilt is small enough to frame. Make one for each of the graduates in your household.

Featured Techniques

- recycled fabrics
- clear vinyl pocket
- embellishing with recognition pins

Other Themes

First Communion or Confirmation

Bar Mitzvah or Bat Mitzvah

Scout or service club awards

Special achievement

24½" x 38½" (62.5 x 98 cm). Made by Sandy Bonsib, Issaquah, Washington, 2003. Quilted by Becky Kraus.

Fabric

Note: Use fabrics that are at least 42" (106.5 cm) wide. Use 100% cotton fabrics except where noted.

½ yd. (0.5 m) polyester satin

½ yd. (0.5 m) for binding

⅞ yd. (0.8 m) backing

Materials

Graduation gown and cap

Thread to match satin

Thread to match cap

8" x 10" (20.5 x 25.5 cm) senior photo

8¾" x 10¾" (22 x 27.5 cm) clear vinyl

29" x 43" (74 x 109 cm) cotton batting

Nine recognition pins

Pearl cotton

Crewel needle

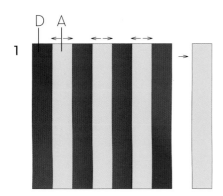

CUTTING

Satin

Cut four strips 2½" x 14½" (6.5 x 37 cm) (A).

Cut nine small squares 2½" x 2½" (6.5 x 6.5 cm) (B).

Cut one large square 14½" x 14½" (37 x 37 cm) (C).

Graduation Gown

Spread out the graduation gown so that you can cut from a flat, single layer of fabric. Cut the gown apart at the seams if needed.

Cut four strips 2½" x 14½" (6.5 x 37 cm) (D).

Cut ten squares 2½" x 2½" (6.5 x 6.5 cm) (E).

Cut two rectangles 4½" x 14½" (11.5 x 37 cm) (F).

Cut two rectangles 4½" x 38½" (11.5 x 98 cm) (G).

ASSEMBLY

Note: Sew all pieces using a ¼" (0.75 cm) seam allowance.

1. Arrange four A and four D strips side by side, alternating the colors as shown. Stitch together. Press toward D (arrows).

Tip: *Sewing slippery polyester satin fabrics can be challenging. For good results, use more pins than usual and make a conscious effort to slow down. Test your iron temperature on scrap fabric. The cotton setting quilters usually use is too hot for the polyester fabrics in this project.*

2

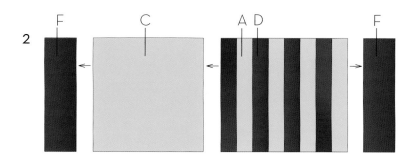

2. Sew C to the left edge of the AD unit. Make sure that the colors continue to alternate. Press. Add an F at each end. Press.

Tip: *If the quilt will not be framed, add a sleeve to the back for hanging (page 14).*

3. Arrange nine B and ten E squares in a row, beginning and ending with E. Stitch together. Press.

3

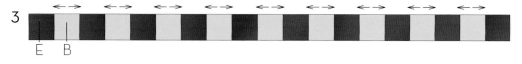

E   B

4. Join the BE unit to the bottom edge of the ADCF unit, as shown in the quilt diagram. Note how the colors alternate, checkerboard-style, where the squares and rectangles meet. Press toward the larger unit. Join G to the top and bottom edges. Press toward G.

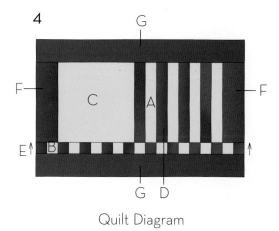

Quilt Diagram

5. Layer the quilt top, batting, and backing. Quilt and bind as desired.

6. Center the clear vinyl rectangle on C. Set the machine for a long stitch length. Stitch around three sides of the rectangle, ¼" (0.75 cm) from the edge, backtacking near the top edge for added reinforcement. Leave the top edge open. Slip the photo into the vinyl pocket.

6

Clear Vinyl "Pocket" with Backtack at Top Edges

7. Attach a recognition pin to the center of each B square, or as desired, depending on the number of pins being displayed. Center the cap on the striped section to the right of the photo pocket. Hand-tack, using pearl cotton and a crewel needle. Tack the tassel to one side so that it doesn't hide the pins.

To Grandpa at Eighty
Message Quilt to Mark a Milestone Birthday

The messages on this quilt were written by members of my family at the 80th birthday party of our beloved dad and grandfather, Carl Brandt. If you don't have enough message blocks for a complete layout, fill in with an appliqué, such as the solo heart seen at the lower right.

Featured Techniques

- group quilt
- signature blocks
- pocket appliqué (page 12)
- on-point blocks

57½" x 69½" (146.5 x 177 cm). Made by Sandy Bonsib, Issaquah, Washington, 1998. Quilted by Becky Kraus.

Fabric

Note: Use fabrics that are at least 42" (106.5 cm) wide.

¼ yd. (0.3 m) each of nine assorted light and medium blues (or use scraps from your stash)

1⅜ yd. (1.3 m) dark blue batik for setting triangles

1½ yd. (1.4 m) medium blue plaid for border

⅝ yd. (0.6 m) white for signature blocks

⅜ yd. (0.4 m) dark blue plaid

½ yd. (0.5 m) for binding

3½ yd. (3.2 m) backing

Materials

Permanent fine-point pens (.5mm or .8mm)

Black fine-grit (#400) wet-dry sandpaper

Template plastic for template

Thread to match heart appliqué

CUTTING

Assorted Blues
Cut two squares 5" x 5" (13 x 13 cm) from each fabric, or 18 squares total. Cut diagonally in half to make 36 triangles (D).
Cut two squares 5" x 5" (13 x 13 cm) from one fabric for the heart appliqué (B).

Dark Blue Batik
Cut two squares 22" x 22" (56 x 56 cm). Cut the squares diagonally in half in both directions for eight triangles. You will use six (E).
Cut two squares 22" x 22" (56 x 56 cm). Cut the squares diagonally in half for four triangles (F).

Medium Blue Plaid
Cut two strips 8½" x 53½" (22 x 136 cm), piecing as needed (G).
Cut two strips 8½" x 57½" (22 x 146.5 cm), piecing as needed (H).

White
Cut 17 squares 6" x 6" (15.5 x 15.5 cm) (A).

Dark Blue Plaid
Cut 16 squares 5" x 5" (13 x 13 cm). Cut the squares diagonally in half to make 32 triangles (C).

ASSEMBLY

Note: Sew all pieces using a ¼" (0.75 cm) seam allowance.

1. Place a white square A on sandpaper to prevent shifting. Write a message on the fabric with a fine-point permanent pen. Keep the writing at least ½" (1.5 cm) from the edges all around. Have friends and family sign 16 A squares total.

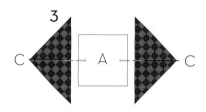

Tip: People will want their block to be perfect. Give them 6" x 6" (15.5 x 15.5 cm) pieces of scrap paper so that they can practice their writing and spacing before writing on fabric. Another option is to have everyone work on paper and then make photo transfers onto fabric. People of all ages will be able to submit their best design and discard the squares they don't like.

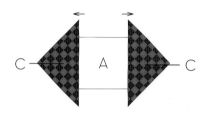

2. Make a template of the heart pattern (page 126). Use the template to make a heart pocket appliqué from the B squares. Center the appliqué on the remaining white A square. Sew in place by hand or machine.

3. Mark the midpoint of each edge of a signed square A. Mark the midpoint of the long edge of four C triangles. Sew two C triangles to the side edges of A, right sides together and midpoints matching. Press toward C (arrows). Trim as shown. Sew two C triangles to the top and bottom edges of A in the same way. Trim to 8½" x 8½" (22 x 22 cm). Make eight AC blocks total.

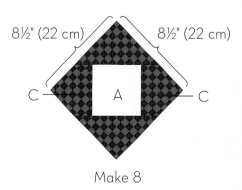

Make 8

4

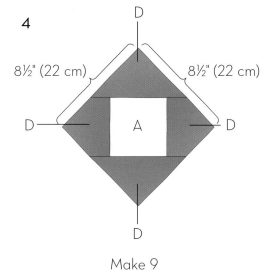

8½" (22 cm)   8½" (22 cm)

Make 9

4. Repeat step 3, using the D triangles and remaining A squares (eight signed and one appliqué) to make nine AD blocks. Be sure all the D triangles in a single block are the same fabric.

5. Arrange the AC signature blocks on point in two columns, as shown in the quilt photo (page 76) and block layout diagram. Place the AD signature blocks on point in between, in three columns. Place the AD heart block at the lower right.

5

Block Layout

6. Place six E setting triangles around the edges, as shown in the quilt assembly diagram. Place an F triangle at each corner. Sew the blocks and setting triangles in diagonal rows. Press as desired. Trim the excess triangle fabric even with the edges of the blocks. Sew the rows together. Press. Add the corner blocks last. Press. Trim the quilt top to 41½" x 53½" (105.5 x 136 cm), or about 4½" (11.5 cm) from the points of the blocks all around.

Tip: Oversized setting triangles create a built-in border. They make the signature and heart blocks look as if they are floating in the dark blue background.

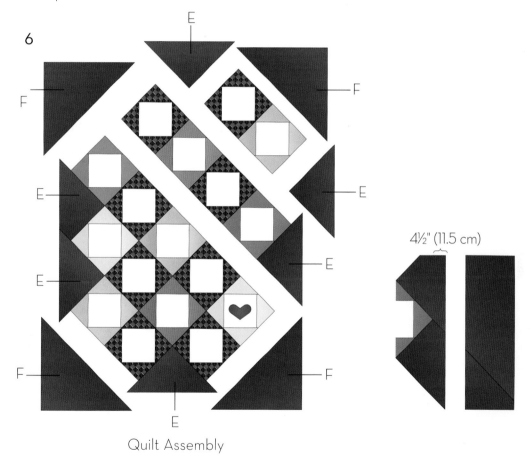

Quilt Assembly

7. Sew the G borders to the side edges of the quilt top. Press toward G. Sew the H borders to the top and bottom edges of the quilt top. Press toward H.

8. Layer the quilt top, batting, and backing. Quilt and bind as desired.

Walking Down the Aisle

A Pillow for a Favorite Wedding Photograph

At age sixty-two, my mother married Carl Brandt. Mom's dream was to be married in a white wedding dress because her first wedding day had been much less formal. Mom and Carl had a storybook love affair and were married almost twenty years. I made this pillow a few months after she died and gave it to Dad for his 85th birthday, hoping it would be a way for him to "hug" her. The joy this pillow brought him for the rest of his life amazed me. He proudly displayed it and showed it to everyone, and it was with him the day he died. It is now owned by Carl's granddaughter and my niece, Paige Magley.

Featured Techniques

- photo transfer (page 8)
- removable pillow cover

19½" x 19½" (49.5 x 49.5 cm). Made and quilted by Sandy Bonsib, Issaquah, Washington, 2003.

Fabric

Note: Use fabrics that are at least 42" (106.5 cm) wide. Choose colors that coordinate with the wedding photo.

¼ yd. (0.3 m) white for photo transfer

½ yd. (0.5 m) medium or dark plaid

⅜ yd. (0.4 m) light stripe

⅝ yd. (0.6 m) for quilt backing

⅝ yd. (0.6 m) for pillow backing

Materials

8" x 10" (20.5 x 25.5 cm) wedding picture

Photo transfer paper

Thread to match pillow backing

24" x 24" (61 x 61 cm) cotton batting

20" x 20" (51 x 51 cm) pillow form

Point turner

CUTTING

Medium or Dark
Cut two squares 16½" x 16½" (42 x 42 cm). Cut diagonally in half to make four triangles (B).

Light
Cut two squares 10½" x 10½" (27 x 27 cm). Cut diagonally in half to make four triangles (A).

Pillow Backing
Cut two rectangles 18" x 20" (46 x 51 cm) (C).

ASSEMBLY

Note: Sew all pieces using a ¼" (0.75 cm) seam allowance.

1. Review the manufacturer instructions for your photo transfer paper. Resize your photo to 7" x 9" (18 x 23 cm) and make a photo transfer onto white fabric. Cut out the transfer ¼" (0.75 cm) beyond the image outline.

2. Mark the midpoint of the long edge of each A triangle. Mark the midpoint of each edge of the photo transfer. Sew two A triangles to the side edges of the photo transfer, right sides together and midpoints matching. Press toward A (arrows). Trim as shown.

3. Sew two A triangles to the remaining edges of the photo transfer. Press. Turn the unit on-point. Trim to 13½" x 13½" (34.5 x 34.5 cm), with the photo centered.

2

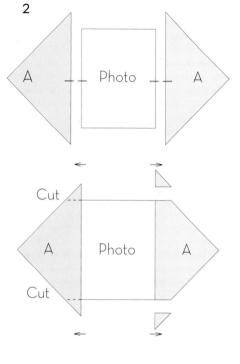

3

13½" (34.5 cm)　　　13½" (34.5 cm)

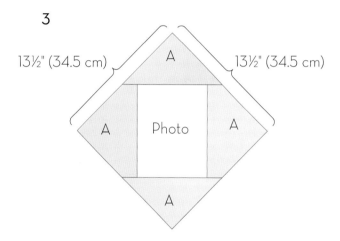

4. Mark the midpoint of the long edge of each B triangle. Mark the midpoint of each edge of the photo transfer unit. Sew two B triangles to opposite edges of the unit, right sides together and midpoints matching. Press toward B. Repeat to join the remaining two B triangles. Trim to 20" x 20" (51 x 51 cm) with the photo central.

4　20" (51 cm)

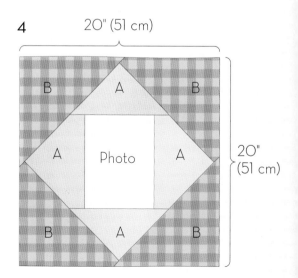

20" (51 cm)

5. Layer the pillow top, batting, and backing. Quilt ¼" (0.75 cm) from each seam line. Do not bind.

Tip: *Quilting around the photo helps it pop out.*

6. Fold in the 18" (46 cm) edge of C 4" (10 cm). Press. Tuck in the raw edge until it meets the fold line and press again, for a 2" (5 cm) double fold. Stitch ⅛" (0.3 cm) from the second fold through all layers with matching thread. Make two.

6 2" (5 cm)

Right Side — — Wrong Side

7. Place C on the quilted pillow top, right sides together. Align the raw edges on three sides. Align the second C over the exposed area, so that the folded edges overlap and the entire pillow top is covered. Stitch ¼" (0.75 cm) from the edge all around.

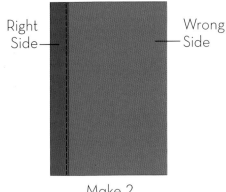

Right Side — — Wrong Side

Make 2

7

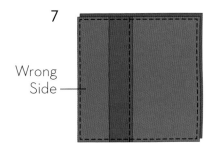

Wrong Side —

8. Turn the pillow cover right sides out. Use a point turner to poke out the corners. Insert the pillow form through the opening at the back. Leave the opening unstitched so that the pillow cover can be easily removed for laundering.

Tip: *Size a pillow cover ½" (1.5 cm) smaller than the pillow form. For a 20" x 20" (51 x 51 cm) pillow form, make a 19½" x 19½" (49.5 x 49.5 cm) cover. The form will fit snugly inside the cover, for a full, round, plump look.*

eph's Indian School

Recognizes

Mr. Osmon T. Nelson

a standing member in the

TIPI PRESS CLUB

ipi Press Club promotes the history, beliefs, legends and customs of the Lakota p
Our focus is in instill in Native American Youth pride in their roots as well as
all people the opportunity to learn more about Lakota and Native American heri
the medium of Art and Literature.

Remembering

Those We Loved

He Loved to Fish

A Memorial Quilt about Favorite Pastimes

Linda Nelson made this quilt in memory of her father-in-law, O.T. Nelson. It focuses on his love of fishing. Two plaid shirts, a cloth hat, and a photo transfer—proof of a good catch—are among the items stitched to the surface. The shirt backs were cut off to reduce bulk as well as provide extra fabric for the fish pocket appliqués.

Techniques to Try

- photo transfer (page 8)

- clothing as appliqué

- pocket appliqué (page 12)

- recycled patchwork blocks

65½" x 70½" (166.5 x 179.5 cm). Made and quilted by Linda Nelson, Clinton, Washington, 2003.

Fabric
Note: Use fabrics that are at least 42" (106.5 cm) wide.

¼ yd. (0.3 m) white for photo transfers

½ yd. (0.5 m) each of 10 to 15 assorted light neutrals

⅛ yd. (0.2 m) soft green flannel

Scrap of tan plaid

⅝ yd. (0.6 m) for binding

4 yd. (3.7 m) backing

Materials
Photograph

Certificate

Photo transfer paper

Two wool plaid shirts

Soft fabric hat

Pearl cotton

Chenille needle

Fine-point permanent marker

70" x 75" (178 x 190.5 cm) batting

Template plastic for templates

CUTTING

Assorted Light Neutrals
Cut 20 rectangles 13½" x 18" (34.5 x 46 cm). To substitute patchwork you have on hand, see the tip under step 2.

Tan Plaid
Cut a small six-sided shape for the quilt label.

The appliqués are cut in steps 4 and 5.

ASSEMBLY

Note: Sew all pieces using a ¼" (0.75 cm) seam allowance.

1. Review the manufacturer instructions for your photo transfer paper. Copy the photo and certificate and make photo transfers onto white fabric. Cut out each transfer ¼" (0.75 cm) beyond the image outline.

2. Arrange the light neutral rectangles in a 4 x 5 grid, as shown in the quilt photo (page 88). Stitch the rectangles together in rows. Press the seams in adjacent rows in opposite directions. Sew the rows together. Press.

Tip: *If you have scraps of patchwork from a past project or an unfinished quilt, here's your chance to showcase them. In this quilt, the second block from the left was cut from a piece of leftover checkerboard patchwork.*

3. Arrange the plaid shirts, soft hat, photo transfers, and quilt label on the pieced background, as shown in the quilt photo (page 88). Trim out part of the back of each shirt to reduce the bulk.

4. Make a template for each fish pattern. Use the fish templates to make four pocket appliqués (see page 126) from the cutaway plaids.

5. Arrange the fish appliqués on the quilt top, just below the shirts. Cut and add a plaid strip above the fish, a long green flannel strip for the fishing pole, and a shorter plaid strip for the pole handle. Set aside the remaining plaid for the second side of the quilt.

3

5

6. Appliqué the assembled collage to the quilt top by hand or machine. Raw edges can be turned under or zigzagged. Thread a chenille needle with pearl cotton. Embroider a long fishing line and hook in backstitch or as desired. Use a marking pen to sign the label.

7. Layer the quilt top, batting, and backing. Quilt and bind as desired.

A Watercolor Memory

A Memory Quilt Featuring Someone's Artwork or Photography

My mother, Joan Brandt, died in January 2003 at the age of eighty-one. When she was alive, she found little time for hobbies but did allow herself time to "take lessons" from her father, Louis W. Bonsib, a famous Indiana watercolor and oil painting landscape artist. I always thought this was a wonderful way for the two of them to spend time together. When Mom died, her brushes and this watercolor painting were given to me. To display this small collection, I pieced together a fabric background in a similar palette. A clear acrylic pocket protects the painting. Mom's brushes are couched to the quilt, forming a unique frame around it.

Featured Techniques

- clear vinyl pocket
- embellishing with artist's brushes

Other Themes

The house where you grew up

Baby's or newlyweds' first Christmas

Professions

Hobbies

36½" x 42" (93 x 107 cm). Made by Sandy Bonsib, Issaquah, Washington, 2003. Quilted by Becky Kraus.

Fabric

Note: Use fabrics that are 42" (106.5 cm) wide unless noted. Search through your stash for fabric colors and textures that coordinate with your watercolor painting or other display item. Use medium values for the interior blocks and dark values for the border.

Thirteen assorted fabric pieces

½ yd. (0.5 m) for binding

1⅜ yd. (1.3 m) backing

Materials

41" x 46" (104 x 117 cm) batting

16" x 20" (40.5 x 51 cm) matted watercolor

17" x 21" (43 x 53.5 cm) clear vinyl

Eleven artist's paintbrushes

Pearl cotton

Chenille needle

CUTTING

Refer to the quilt diagram (opposite).

Medium Values
Cut 11 rectangles, each from a different fabric:
5½" x 18" (14.5 x 46 cm) (A)
5½" x 7½" (14.5 x 19.5) (B)
7½" x 17½" (19.5 x 44.5 cm) (C)
11" x 16½" (28.5 x 42 cm) (D)
6½" x 11" (16.5 x 28.5) (E)
7" x 18" (18 x 46 cm) (F)
3½" x 18" (9 x 46 cm) (G)
12¼" x 13" (31.5 x 33.5 cm) (H)
12" x 13" (30.5 x 33.5 cm) (I)
6" x 13" (15.5 x 33.5 cm) (J)
8¼" x 13" (21.5 x 33.5 cm) (K)

Dark Values
Cut four strips. Use one fabric for L and another fabric for M, N, and O:
4" x 37" (10.5 x 94.5 cm) (L)
3" x 36½" (8 x 93 cm) (M)
3" x 37" (8 x 94.5 cm) (N)
3" x 36½" (8 x 93 cm) (O)

ASSEMBLY

Note: Sew all pieces using a ¼" (0.75 cm) seam allowance. Press seams as desired.

1. Arrange pieces A through O as shown in the quilt diagram.

2. Sew B to C. Press. Sew D to E. Press. Sew BC to DE. Press. Join pieces A, F, and G to this unit to complete one row. Press.

3. Join pieces H, I, J, and K to complete another row. Press. Join the two rows together. Press. Add borders N and L. Press. Add borders M and O. Press.

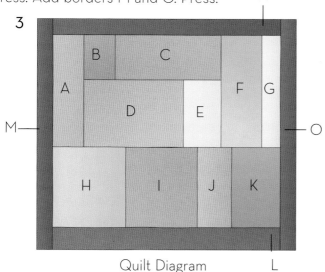

Quilt Diagram

> *Tip:* Make a patchwork background larger or smaller as needed to create an appropriate "frame" for your display piece. Unfortunately, there is no set formula—the proportions can vary. Learn to trust your eye. If the background patchwork looks too big or too small for the display piece, it probably is.

4. Layer the quilt top, batting, and backing. Quilt and bind as desired.

5. Center the clear vinyl on the quilt. Set the machine for a long stitch length. Stitch around three sides of the rectangle, ¼" (0.75 cm) from the edge, backtacking near the top edge for added reinforcement. Leave the top edge open. Slip the painting into the vinyl pocket.

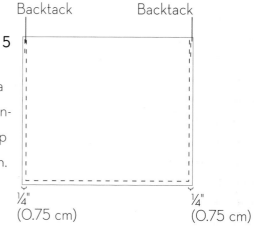

Backtack   Backtack

¼" (0.75 cm)   ¼" (0.75 cm)

6. Arrange the paintbrushes on the quilt end to end, forming a 22" x 26" (56 x 66 cm) rectangle around the painting. Thread a chenille needle with pearl cotton. Couch each brush to the surface.

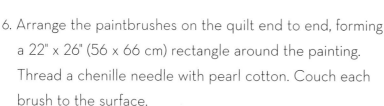

Stitching

A Letter from Gwen, One Loyal, Loving Lab

To my Best Friend John

I came to live with you when I was a pup. I was the runt of the litter and was just a couple of months old. You're the best friend a dog could ever have. I rode "shotgun" for you for the rest of my life, and what a life it was! We lived all over the country! We went to college together, got married (I was your Best Dog), honeymooned in Park City, bought a house and raised Ben and Kate.

Remember all the hikes we took? And I loved sailing on the Chesapeake Bay with you in your boat. How about the time I saved your life by licking your cheek when you passed out in the snow in Colorado? I'm so glad I decided to come home that day! We had so many great and wonderful adventures together....

You always said I was one of the best things that ever happened to you, And you were the most important person in my life. Gosh, you were my life!

Everyone was my friend. Sometimes, when you went into a store, I'd get out of the car and wait for you at the door. Everybody coming out of the store would talk to me, but I never took my eyes off the door until you came out.

I'm sorry I couldn't stay longer, but we were lucky to have each other for 14 years. And I'll still be waiting and watching at the door until I see you coming through. I love you.

Gwen

Our Wonderful Lab
Memory Quilt about a Pet

When I met my husband more than twenty years ago, Gwen, his Labrador retriever, was his constant companion. She accompanied him everywhere, including camping trips (where this photo was taken) and his college classes. Gwen was "Best Dog" at our wedding and continued to enjoy good health until our children were three and five years old. At the ripe old age of fourteen, Gwen peacefully died. Some years later, I read an article about a faithful Lab and his adventures with the man he loved. Inspired, I wrote Gwen's story, transferred my text and Gwen's photo to fabric, and assembled the quilt.

Featured Techniques

- photo transfer (page 8)
- sew-and-flip (page 12)
- embellishing with dog biscuits

20½" x 29½" (52 x 75 cm). Made by Sandy Bonsib, Issaquah, Washington, 1998. Quilted by Becky Kraus.

Fabric

Note: Use fabrics that are at least 42" (106.5 cm) wide.

¼ yd. (0.3 m) white for photo transfer

⅜ yd. (0.4 m) yellow for text and frames

⅛ yd. (0.2 m) each of six assorted medium and dark reds

¼ yd. (0.3 m) medium red for frame and binding

¾ yd. (0.7 m) backing

Materials

Computer and printer

Pet photo

Seam ripper

25" x 34" (63.5 x 86.5 cm) batting

18 dog biscuits

Varnish

Brush

Pearl cotton

Chenille needle

CUTTING

Yellow

Cut two squares 2" x 2" (5 x 5 cm) (A).

Cut two strips 2" x 8½" (5.5 x 22 cm) (B).

Cut one strip 1½" x 10" (4 x 25.5 cm) (C).

Cut two squares 2⅞ " x 2⅞" (7.5 x 7.5 cm). Cut diagonally in half to make four triangles (E).

Cut two strips 2" x 11" (5.5 x 28 cm) (F).

Cut two strips 2" x 21½" (5.5 x 54.5 cm) (G).

Set aside the remaining yellow for text photo transfer, step 1.

Assorted Reds

Cut one strip 2½" x 42" (6.5 x 106.5 cm) from each fabric, or six strips total (I).

Medium Red

Cut two strips 1" x 42" (3 x 106.5 cm) (D).

Cut four squares 3" x 3" (7.5 x 7.5 cm) (H).

ASSEMBLY

Note: Sew all pieces using a ¼" (0.75 cm) seam allowance.

1. Create a computer file, select a font, and type your pet's story, using about 250 words. Arrange the text in two columns. Print the text onto plain paper. Review the manufacturer instructions for your photo transfer paper. Copy your story text and make a photo

transfer onto yellow fabric. Trim to 10" x 8½" (25.5 x 22 cm), with the text centered and long edges running horizontally.

2. Enlarge your pet photo to 6½" x 8" (16.5 x 20.5 cm). Make a photo transfer onto white fabric. Cut out the transfer ¼" (0.75 cm) beyond the image outline.

Tip: *When you enlarge an image, do a test print on plain paper to make sure the size is accurate. Then print the image on transfer paper.*

3. Sew-and-flip one A square to each top corner of the dog photo transfer. Sew a B strip to each side edge. Press toward B. Sew C to the top edge. Press toward C. Sew the yellow text panel to the bottom edge. Press toward the text.

4. At the top left corner, measure 1¾" (4.5 cm) from the diagonal seam and draw a parallel diagonal line. Cut on the diagonal line. Repeat at the top right corner. Use one of the cutoff triangles as a template to cut the bottom corners to match.

5. Align a D strip on the lower right diagonal edge of the block unit. Stitch together through both layers. Press toward D (arrows). Trim off the excess D even with the block unit. Repeat this process, adding eight D strips around the entire block in the order shown. Press and trim after each addition.

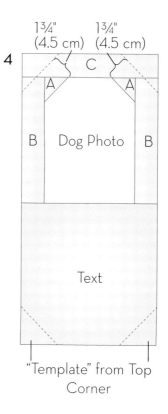

"Template" from Top Corner

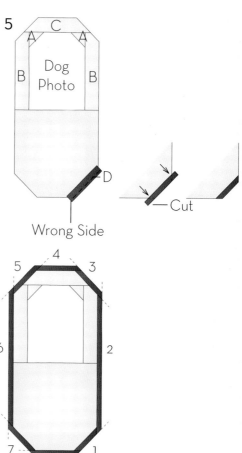

Wrong Side

6. Sew an E triangle to each corner of the block unit. Press toward E. Sew an F strip to the top and bottom edges. Press toward F. Sew a G strip to each side edge. Press toward G. Sew-and-flip an H square to each corner. Press.

7. Arrange the six assorted I strips side by side. Sew the long edges together. Press as desired. Cut the strip set into eight segments 4" (10.5 cm) wide.

4" (10.5 cm)

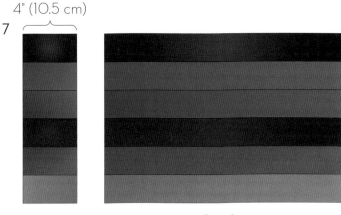

Cut 8

8. Piece two segments end to end. Make four units. Use a seam ripper to remove one rectangle each from two units. Sew these strips to the sides of the quilt top. Press as desired. Remove two rectangles each from the remaining two units. Sew to top and bottom edges of the quilt top. Press.

9. Layer the quilt top, batting, and backing. Quilt as desired. Bind with medium red fabric.

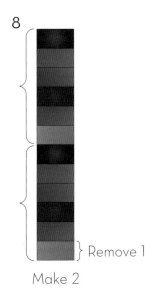

} Remove 1

Make 2

A Letter from Gwen, One Loyal, Loving Lab

To my Best Friend John

I came to live with you when I was a pup. I was the runt of the litter and was just a couple of months old. You're the best friend a dog could ever have. I rode "shotgun" for you for the rest of my life, and what a life it was! We lived all over the country! We went to college together, got married (I was your Best Dog), honeymooned in Park City, bought a house and raised Ben and Kate.

Remember all the hikes we took? And I loved sailing on the Chesapeake Bay with you in your boat. How about the time I saved your life by licking your cheek when you passed out in the snow in Colorado? I'm so glad I decided to come home that day! We had so many great and wonderful adventures together….

You always said I was one of the best things that ever happened to you. And you were the most important person in my life. Gosh, you were my life!

Everyone was my friend. Sometimes, when you went into a store, I'd get out of the car and wait for you at the door. Everybody coming out of the store would talk to me, but I never took my eyes off the door until you came out.

I'm sorry I couldn't stay longer, but we were lucky to have each other for 14 years. And I'll still be waiting and watching at the door until I see you coming through. I love you.

Gwen

10. Brush varnish on 18 dog biscuits. Let dry overnight. Tack dog biscuits to alternate border rectangles using a chenille needle and pearl cotton.

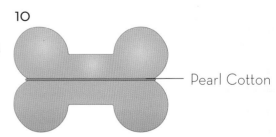

10

Pearl Cotton

Four Generations of Women
Family History Quilt with Photographs and Heirlooms

This quilt uses photographs and embellishments to document four generations of women in the same family: quiltmaker Sue Van Gerpen; her mother, Sue DeVito; her grandmother, Jeanette Ettswold; and her great-grandmothers Myrtle Sommers and Anna Sommers. Myrtle married, bore a child, and died young. Her husband then married Anna, who bore Jeannette. The quilt is richly embellished with photo transfers of all five women, picture frames created from lace trim, Grandma's crocheted coin purse, border strips cut from a corset bag, and many other vintage items.

Featured Techniques

- photo transfer (page 8)
- recycled fabrics
- embellishing with vintage buttons and memorabilia

51½" x 63½" (131 x 161.5 cm). Made by Sue Van Gerpen, North Bend, Washington, 1998. Quilted by Becky Kraus.

Fabric

Note: Use fabrics that are at least 42" (106.5 cm) wide.

1 yd. (0.9 m) white for photo transfers

½ yd. (0.5 m) total assorted neutrals (or use scraps from your stash)

⅜ yd. (0.4 m) each of four assorted light neutrals

⅜ yd. (0.4 m) each of four assorted medium neutrals

½ yd. (0.5 m) for binding

3¼ yd. (3 m) backing

Materials

Twenty photographs in various sizes

Light-colored vintage garment bags, linens, or other textiles, at least 8" (20.5 cm) wide

56" x 68" (142 x 173 cm) batting

Assorted bits of lace

Lace-edged handkerchief

Satin coin purse

Vintage buttons

CUTTING

Assorted Neutrals

Choose four different mediums or darks. From each fabric, cut one square 3½" x 3½" (9 x 9 cm) (A) and four squares 2" x 2" (5.5 x 5.5 cm) (B).

Choose four different lights. From each fabric, cut four rectangles 2" x 3½" (5.5 x 9 cm) (C).

Cut 20 assorted strips 2" x 21" (5.5 x 53.5 cm), or longer if possible (D). Shorter lengths can be pieced together end to end as needed.

Cut 32 assorted squares 2" x 2" (5.5 x 5.5 cm) (E). The E squares may be cut from the D strips.

Cut 32 assorted squares 2⅜" x 2⅜" (6.5 x 6.5 cm). Cut diagonally in half for 64 triangles (F).

Light and Medium Neutrals

From light neutrals, cut four different 7¼" x 7¼" (18.5 x 18.5 cm) squares. Cut diagonally in half in both directions for 16 triangles (G).

Cut one square 12½" x 12½" (32 x 32 cm) from each fabric, or eight squares total (H).

Light Vintage Textiles

Cut into pieces 8" (20.5 cm) wide and as long as possible, until the total length is at least 170" (432 cm) (I).

ASSEMBLY

Note: Sew all pieces using a ¼" (0.75 cm) seam allowance.

1. Review the manufacturer instructions for your photo transfer paper. Copy your photos and make photo transfers onto white fabric. Cut out each transfer ¼" (0.75 cm) beyond the image outline.

2. Arrange one A, four B, and four C as shown; note that A and B are cut from one fabric. Stitch the pieces together in rows. Press the middle row toward A. Press the top and bottom rows toward B. Make four blocks.

3. Sew two D strips together. Press toward the darker fabric. Make ten assorted strip sets. Cut into segments 2" (5.5 cm) wide. Sew 32 segments together in pairs to make 16 Four-Patch units. Set the remaining D segments aside.

2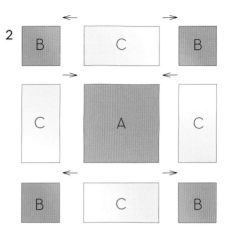

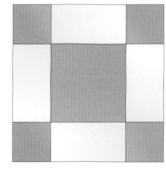

Make 4

3

Cut 2" (5.5 cm) Segments
Strip Set: Make 10 Assorted

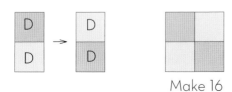

Make 16

4

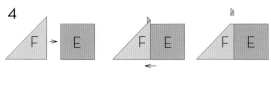

4. Sew an F triangle to the left edge of square E. Press toward F. Trim as shown. Sew another F triangle to the top edge of E. Press. Make 32 EF units.

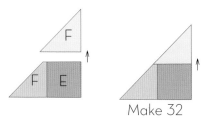

Make 32

5. Sew the long edge of EF to a short edge of G. Press toward G. Join another EF to G. Press toward G. Make 16 EFG units.

6

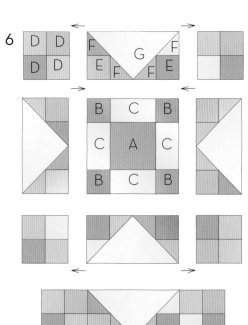

Make 4

5

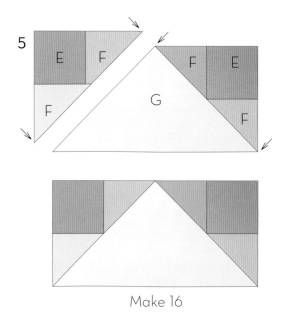

Make 16

6. Arrange one ABC unit, four Four-Patch units, and four EFG units as shown. Sew the units together in rows. Press the middle row toward ABC. Press the top and bottom rows toward the Four-Patch units. Make four blocks, each 12½" x 12½" (32 x 32 cm).

7. Arrange four pieced blocks and eight H blocks in four rows, as shown in the quilt photo (page 102). Sew the blocks together in rows. Press the seams in opposite directions from row to row. Join the rows. Press.

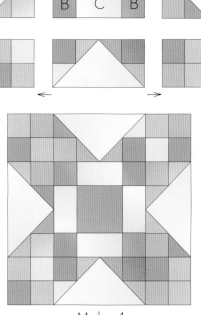

8. Arrange 12 D segments from step 3 and one extra D square in a 5 x 5 grid. Join and press the segments as shown to make four corner blocks.

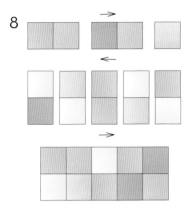

9. Lay out the I border pieces around the quilt top in a pleasing pattern. Join the pieces for each border end to end. Press as desired. Trim the side borders to 8" x 48½" (20.5 x 123.5 cm). Join them to the quilt top. Press toward I. Trim the top and bottom borders to 8" x 36½" (20.5 x 93 cm). Sew a D block to each end. Press toward I. Join the border to the quilt top. Press.

10. Arrange the photos from step 1 at various angles on the plain blocks of the quilt top. Appliqué in place. Sew a handkerchief, coin purse, buttons, lace, and other memorabilia to the surface. Some pieces may be easier to attach after the quilting is complete.

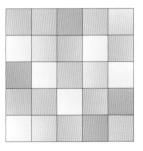

Make 4

Tip: To give photos a framed look, sew fabric strips or lace around the edges. Oval photos can be appliquéd to a fabric background.

11. Layer the quilt top, batting, and backing. Quilt and bind as desired.

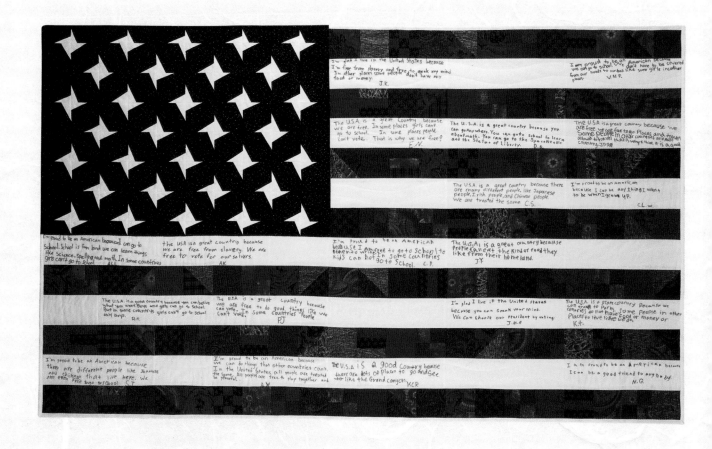

I'm glad I live in the United States because I'm free from slavery and free to speak my mind. In other places some people don't have any food or money. J.K.

I am proud to be an American because we can go to school. We don't have to be covered from our heads to ourtoes like some girls in other places. V.M.F.

The U.S.A. is a great country because we are free. In some places girls cant go to school. In some places people can't vote. That is why we are free? F.N.

The U.S.A. is a great country because you can go anywhere. You can go to school to learn about math. You can go to the SpaceNeedle and the Statue of Liberty. D.S.

The U.S.A is a great country because we are free. We are free to go Places and travel. Some people in other countries are not allowed to travel that's why I think it is a good country. J.D.R.

The U.S.A. is a great country because there are many different people, like Japanese people, Irish people, and Chinese people. We are treated the same. C.S.

I'm proud to be an American because I can be anything I want to be when I grow up. C.L.W.

I'm proud to be an American because I can go to School. School is fun and we can learn things like Science, Spelling and math, In some countries girls can't go to school. A.L.

the USA is a great country because we are free from slavery. We are free to vote for ourselves. A.K.

I'm proud to be an American because I AM free to go to School to kids can not in some countries go to School. C.P.

The U.S.A. is a great country because people can eat the kind of food they like from their homeland. J.Y.

The U.S.A. is a good country because you can be buy what you want. Boys and girls can go to school. But in some country's girls can't go to school. R.T.

The U.S.A. is a great country because we are free to do good things like we can vote. In some countries people can't vote. P.J.

I'm glad I live in the United States because you can speak your mind. We can choose our President by voting. J.M.R.

The U.S.A. is a great country Because we can travel to Paris. Some people in other countries do not have food or money or places to live like we do. K.F.

I'm proud to be an American because there are different people like Japanese and chinese that live here. We are even free to go to school. S.T.

I'm proud to be an American because we can do things that other countries can't. In the United States all people are treated the same. All people are free to play together and be peaceful. A.W.

The U.S.A is a good country because there are lots of places to go and see like the Grand canyon. K.C.R.

I am proud to be an American because I can be a good friend to any body! N.G.

America Remembers
Flag Quilt to Honor People or Events

Becky Kraus designed this quilt for an elementary school PTA auction. The signature blocks were written by Ms. Rosenthal's second grade class at the Eastgate Elementary School, Bellevue, Washington. In the aftermath of the September 11, 2001 tragedy, the children were asked to comment on their country or to complete the statement "I am proud to be an American because . . . ." Their reflections cover everything from the abolishment of slavery to girls being allowed to go to school. The children made such thoughtful statements that Becky, the quiltmaker, ended up buying the quilt herself!

Featured Techniques

- quilting with children (page 7)
- signature blocks

66½" x 39½" (169 x 100.5 cm). Made and quilted by Becky Kraus, Bellevue, Washington, 2002.

Fabric

Note: Use fabrics that are at least 42" (106.5 cm) wide.

2 yd. (1.8 m) white for stripes, stars, and binding

2 yd. (1.8 m) total assorted medium and dark reds for stripes

1½ yd. (1.4 m) dark blue for star field and binding

2 yd. (1.8 m) backing

Materials

Blue permanent fine-point markers

Black fine-grit (#400) wet-dry sandpaper

71" x 44" (180.5 x 112 cm) batting

CUTTING

White

Cut 24 rectangles 3½" x 12½" (9 x 32 cm) (A).

Cut three rectangles 3½" x 6½" (9 x 16.5 cm) (B).

Cut 128 rectangles 1½" x 3" (4 x 8 cm) (L).

Set aside the remaining white for the binding.

Assorted Reds

Cut three medium strips (from one fabric) 1½" x 21" (4 x 53.5 cm) (C).

Cut three dark strips (from one fabric) 1½" x 21" (4 x 53.5 cm) (D).

Cut six assorted strips 1½" x 21" (4 x 53.5 cm) (E).

Cut four assorted medium strips 2" x 21" (5.5 x 53.5 cm) (F).

Cut four assorted dark strips 2" x 21" (5.5 x 53.5 cm) (G).

Cut 11 assorted medium squares 3⅞" x 3⅞" (10 x 10 cm). Cut diagonally in half for 22 triangles (H).

Cut 11 assorted dark squares 3⅞" x 3⅞" (10 x 10 cm). Cut diagonally in half for 22 triangles (I).

Cut 58 assorted squares 3½" x 3½" (9 x 9 cm) (J).

Dark Blue

Cut 80 squares 3½" x 3½" (9 x 9 cm) (K).

Set aside the remaining dark blue for the binding.

ASSEMBLY

Note: Sew all pieces using a ¼" (0.75 cm) seam allowance.

1. Place an A rectangle on sandpaper to prevent slipping. Have participants use a blue permanent marker to write "I am proud to be an American because" or "The U.S.A. is a great country because" and then complete the sentence. In the project quilt, 19 A pieces are signed and five are blank. The B pieces were also left blank.

2. Sew two D strips to one C strip. Press toward D. Cut the DCD strip set into eight segments 1½" (4 cm) wide. Sew two C strips to one D strip. Press toward D (arrows). Cut the CDC strip set into four segments 1½" (4 cm) wide. Arrange three segments in a Nine-Patch as shown. Sew together. Press as desired. Make four Nine-Patch blocks.

3. Sew three E strips together. Press toward the darker fabric. Make two strip sets. Cut these strip sets and the remaining DCD and CDC strip sets into segments 3½" (9 cm) wide. Make 14 Rail Fence blocks.

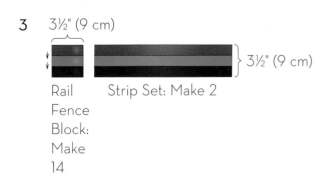

3   3½" (9 cm)
Rail Fence Block: Make 14   Strip Set: Make 2   3½" (9 cm)

More Theme Ideas

This American Remembers pattern has other possibilities.

- A partial list of people who died on September 11 could be written on smaller rectangles.

- When a soldier dies, friends and family on a military base could write messages of remembrance and give this quilt to the soldier's family.

- In a soldier's home town, friends could write messages of remembrance, affection, and encouragement when that soldier leaves for combat and give the quilt to his or her parents for good luck.

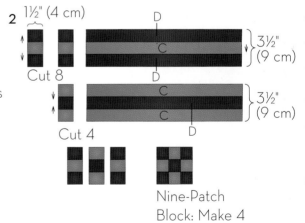

2 1½" (4 cm)   D   3½" (9 cm)   Cut 8   C   D
Cut 4   C   C   D   3½" (9 cm)
Nine-Patch Block: Make 4

4. Sew F to G. Press toward G. Make four strip sets. Cut into 34 segments 2" (5.5 cm) wide. Arrange two segments in a Four-Patch, with the darker G squares diagonally opposite, as shown. Sew together. Press as desired. Make 17 Four-Patch blocks.

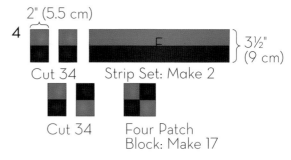

2" (5.5 cm)

4

F

3½" (9 cm)

Cut 34   Strip Set: Make 2

Cut 34   Four Patch Block: Make 17

5. Sew H to I. Press toward I. Make 21 half-square triangles total. (Discard the two remaining triangles.)

6. Arrange the A, B, J, and red pieced blocks in 13 rows as shown. Sew the blocks together in rows. Press alternate rows in opposite directions. Join rows 1 through 7 . Press. Join rows 8 through 13. Press.

5

Half-Square Triangle: Make 21

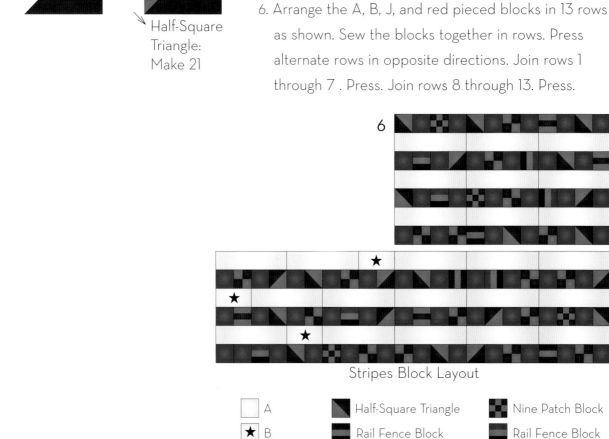

6

Stripes Block Layout

	A		Half-Square Triangle		Nine Patch Block
★	B		Rail Fence Block		Rail Fence Block
	J		Four Patch Block		

7. Sew a white L across one corner of a blue K. Press as shown. Trim L even with K. The angle of the stitching line does not have to be precise and can vary from unit to unit. Make 32 KL units.

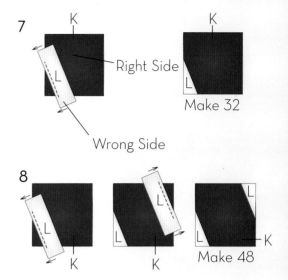

8. Sew two white L pieces to opposite corners of a blue K. Press and trim as shown. Make 48 KLL units.

9. Arrange the KL and KLL units in eight rows, as shown. The KL units fall at the edges. Sew the units together in rows. Press the seams in opposite directions from row to row. Sew the rows together. Press as desired. Trim 1½" (4 cm) off the top and bottom edges, or so the star unit measures 30½" x 21½" (77.5 x 55 cm).

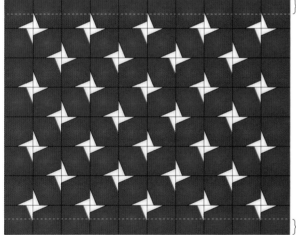

} Cut 1½" (4 cm) Off Top Edge

} Cut 1½" (4 cm) Off Bottom Edge

10. Sew the star unit to the left edge of the shorter stripes unit. Press as desired. Join to the larger stripes unit. Press.

11. Layer the quilt top, batting, and backing. Quilt as desired. Bind with white and blue fabric, as shown in the quilt photo (page 108).

When this you see
Remember me -
My heart I stitch
Here for thee. ♡

When This You See, Remember Me

A Small Quilt Project from Damaged Antique Quilts

This small quilt features fragments of past quilt projects that were rescued by modern-day quiltmaker Carolyn Vallelunga. *When This You See* uses a vintage quilt block that was pieced but never sewn into a quilt. The surrounding strips are reproduction prints. The quilt is embellished with embroidery, buttons, lace, and other items. Simple messages embroidered with large stitches add to the folk art quality. Serendipity is the rule when it comes to recycling old quilts and quilt blocks. Every piece is unique.

Featured Techniques

- recycled quilts
- pearl cotton embroidery
- primitive alphabet to embroider
- embellishing with vintage items

12" x 20½" (30.5 x 52 cm). Made by Carolyn Vallelunga, Aptos, California, 2000, using fragments of antique quilting.

Fabric
Note: Use fabrics that are at least 42" (106.5 cm) wide.

Scraps of 12 to 15 assorted reproduction prints

Scrap of muslin

Materials
Vintage patchwork block, about 7" x 7" (18 x 18 cm)

Scrap of checkerboard patchwork

Five vintage buttons

Embroidery floss ooooor pearl cotton in assorted colors

Chenille needle

16" x 25" (40.5 x 63.5 cm) batting

Stuffing for heart

CUTTING

From muslin, cut one rectangle 7" x 4½" (18 x 11.5 cm) (A) and two rectangles 3" x 4½" (7.5 x 11.5 cm) (C).
From the assorted reproduction prints, cut nine to ten strips 12" to 14" (30.5 to 35.5 cm) long. Vary the strip width.
From a dark reproduction print, cut two strips 1½" x 42" (4 x 106.5 cm) (B).

ASSEMBLY

Note: Sew all pieces using a ¼" (0.75 cm) seam allowance.

1. Refer to the quilt photo and assembly diagram. Arrange the checkerboard patchwork, muslin A, and vintage patchwork as shown. Fill in with various strips, choosing colors and patterns that contrast. Trim long strips as needed to make them more manageable, but don't be concerned with precise lengths at this time.

2. Sew the strips to A and the patchwork block in the numerical order shown. After each addition, press toward the darker fabric. Trim and even up the edges. Make two smaller units and then sew the units together. Trim as needed to square up the corners.

3. Sew B to a side edge of the quilt top. Trim off the excess. Press toward B. Repeat on the opposite side edge and at the top and bottom edges, pressing after each addition.

4. Write a simple saying on the muslin block lightly in pencil, by tracing letters or writing in freehand. For a primitive look, use a combination of uppercase and lowercase letters.

5. Layer the quilt top, batting, and backing. Quilt as desired; save the batting scraps. To accent the patchwork block, thread a chenille needle with three strands of floss or pearl cotton and quilt a running stitch through all the layers. Embroider the hand-lettered message in backstitch or running stitch. Change thread color often to add to the charm. Bind with a strip made from assorted scraps.

6. Place two C muslins right sides together. Draw an elongated heart shape freehand on the top piece. Stitch on the heart outline through both layers. Trim ¼" (0.75 cm) from the stitching all around. Clip the curves. Cut a slit in the middle of the heart through one layer only. Turn right side out. Stuff a small amount of batting into the heart. Hand-sew closed. Sew a button and ribbon bow to the front. Tack the heart and assorted buttons to the quilt top.

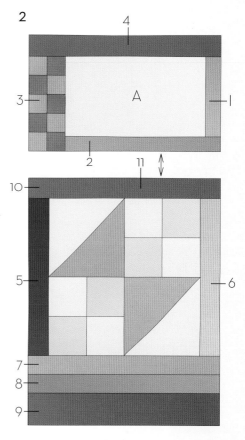

Assembly Diagram

Simple Sayings

Let your heart be glad this day

Live, love, laugh

Love lives here

You make my heart smile

To my dearest friend

Do your best

When this you see, remember me

Forever friends

Peace and plenty

I Love Quilts

A Photo Gallery of the Quilts You've Made

Ribbons sewn to the lower edge of this traditionally styled wall quilt let me display photos of every quilt I ever made. For the most effective display, choose clear, sharp photos with good color. Enlarge the photos if needed, and crop them so only the quilt shows. To increase the display space, just use longer ribbons.

Featured Techniques

- sew-and-flip (page 12)
- patchwork letters
- Churn Dash block
- Cornerstone block
- photo gallery

23" x 53" (58.5 x 135 cm). Made by Sandy Bonsib, Issaquah, Washington, 2003. Quilted by Becky Kraus.

Fabric

Note: Use fabrics that are at least 42" (106.5 cm) wide.

1⅛ yd. (1 m) total assorted creams and tans

¾ yd. (0.7 m) cream-and-tan plaid for Churn Dash blocks

⅜ yd. (0.4 m) large green plaid for Churn Dash blocks

¼ yd. (0.3 m) light stripe for Churn Dash blocks

¼ yd. (0.3 m) total assorted dark reds

¼ yd. (0.3 m) dark red plaid for Cornerstone blocks

⅛ yd. (0.2 m) small green plaid for Churn Dash blocks

⅜ yd. (0.4 m) for binding

1⅝ yd. (1.5 m) backing

Materials

27" x 57" (68.5 x 145 cm) batting

3 yd. (2.7 m) grosgrain ribbon

Fray preventative

Needle

Quilt photos

Novelty paper clips

CUTTING

Assorted Creams and Tans
Cut 94 squares 1½" x 1½" (4 x 4 cm) (A).
Cut one strip 1½" x 11½" (4 x 29.5 cm) (C).
Cut one strip 1½" x 16½" (4 x 42 cm) (D).
Cut one strip 1½" x 31½" (4 x 80 cm) (E).
Cut two strips 1½" x 7½" (4 x 19.5 cm) (F).
Cut two strips ¾" x 33½" (2.5 x 85.5 cm) (G).
Cut two strips 1½" x 8" (4 x 20.5 cm) (H).
Cut two strips 1¾" x 8" (4.5 x 20.5 cm) (I).
Cut 32 rectangles 1½" x 2" (4 x 5.5 cm) (Q).
Cut 32 rectangles 1½" x 4" (4 x 10.5 cm) (R).
Cut and 32 rectangles 1½" x 6" (4 x 15.5 cm) (S).

Cream-and-Tan Plaid
Cut 32 squares 3½" x 3½" (9 x 9 cm) (M).
Cut eight squares 2" x 2" (5.5 x 5.5 cm) (N).

Large Green Plaid
Cut 32 squares 3½" x 3½" (9 x 9 cm) (L).

Light Stripe
Cut two strips 2" x 42" (5.5 x 106.5 cm) (J).

Assorted Dark Reds and Plaids
Cut 84 squares 1½" x 1½" (4 x 4 cm) (B).
Cut eight squares 2" x 2" (5.5 x 5.5 cm) (O).
Cut 96 squares 1½" x 1½" (4 x 4 cm) (P).

Small Green Plaid
Cut two strips 2" x 42" (5.5 x 106.5 cm) (K).

ASSEMBLY

Note: Sew all pieces using a ¼" (0.75 cm) seam allowance.

Middle Panel

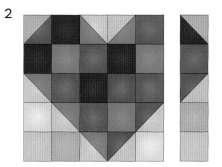

1. Sew-and-flip A and B to make a half-square triangle (page 12). Make 21 AB units.

2. Arrange A and B squares and AB units into a heart shape as shown. Sew the pieces together in vertical rows. Press as desired. Sew the rows together. Press. Repeat to make the letters Q, U, I (make 2), L, T, and S.

2 | B | Letter Fabric | A | Background Fabric | BA | Half-Square Triangle Unit

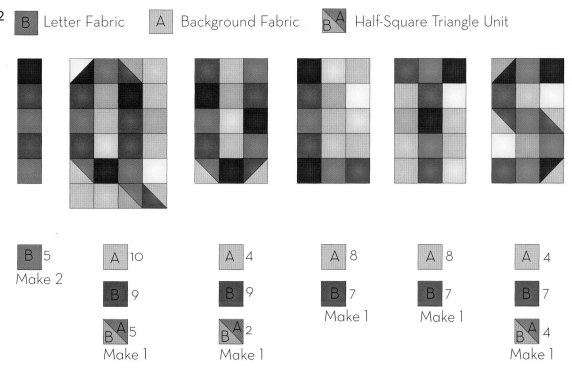

3. Piece five A squares together end to end. Press. Make seven strips total. Arrange the heart shape, a letter I, and four filler strips to spell out I ♥. Sew the pieces together. Press as desired. Sew C to the bottom edge. Press toward C.

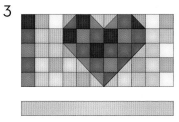

4. Arrange the remaining letters and filler strips to spell UILTS. Note that no filler strip is needed between L and T. Sew the pieces together. Press as desired. Sew D to the bottom edge. Press toward D (arrows). Add the Q.

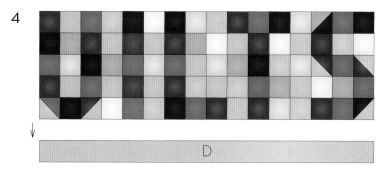

5. Join the units from steps 3 and 4 together. Press as desired. Sew E to the top edge. Press toward E.

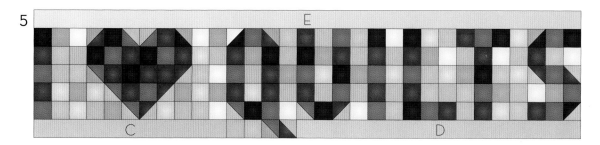

6. Add strip F to each end. Press toward F. Add strip G to the top and bottom edges. Press toward G. Add strip H to each end. Press toward H. Add strip I to each end. Press toward I. The unit should measure 8" x 38" (20.5 x 97 cm).

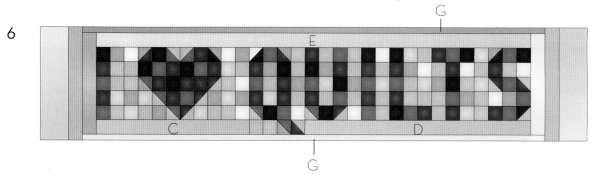

Churn Dash Blocks

1. Sew J and K together. Press toward K. Make two strip sets. Cut into 32 segments 2" (5.5 cm) wide.

2" (5.0 cm)

Cut 32

2. Sew-and-flip (see page 12) L and M together to make a half-square triangle. Make 32.

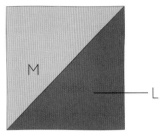

Make 32

3. Arrange four JK, four LM, and one N as shown. Sew the pieces together in rows. Press toward JK. Sew the rows together. Press. Make eight Churn Dash blocks.

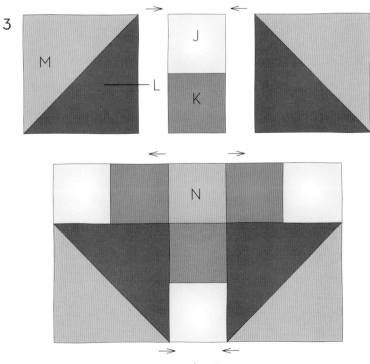

Make 8

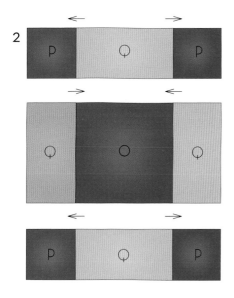

Cornerstone Blocks

1. Sew a P to each end of Q. Press toward P. Make 16 PQP. Repeat to make 16 PRP and 16 PSP.

2. Sew Q to each side edge of O. Press toward O. Sew PQP to the top and bottom edges. Press toward PQP.

3. Sew R to each side edge of the unit. Press toward the unit. Sew PRP to the top and bottom edges. Press toward PRP.

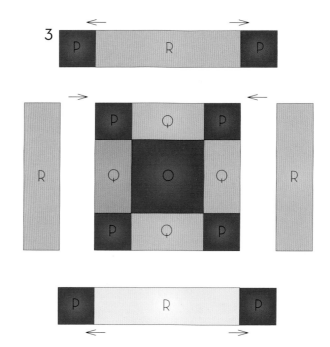

4. Sew S to each side edge of the unit. Press toward the unit. Sew PSP to the top and bottom edges. Press toward PSP. Repeat to make eight Cornerstone blocks.

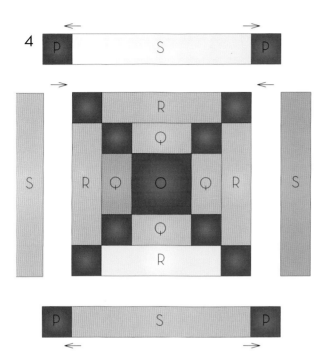

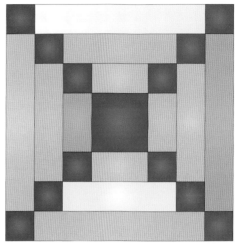

Make 8

FINISHING

1. Arrange the middle panel, Churn Dash blocks, and Cornerstone blocks as shown in the quilt photo (page 118). Sew the pieces together in rows. Press in opposite directions. Join the rows. Press.

2. Layer the quilt top, batting, and backing. Quilt and bind as desired.

3. Cut the ribbon into six pieces, or as desired. Sew the ribbon strips to the bottom edge of the quilt. Seal cut ends with fray preventative, following manufacturer's instructions. Use novelty paper clips to attach quilt photos to the ribbons.

Appliqué Patterns

Enlarge 200%

Look What I Drew
Heart Appliqué

He Loved to Fish
Fish Appliqués

To Grandpa at Eighty
Heart Appliqué

He Loved to Fish
Fish Appliqués

INDEX

ACKNOWLEDGEMENTS

No one ever writes a book alone. It takes the help of many people to make such an undertaking possible.

First of all, I thank my husband for his help, support, and patience through countless tasks, large and small. He is always willing to do anything I ask to get my books to completion.

As I developed the book content, my friends and fellow quilt group members showed me their own quilts. I thank Lynn Ahlers, Linda Nelson, Kathy Staley, and Sue Van Gerpen for their wonderful contributions. Quiltmaker Carolyn Vallelunga contributed the beautiful small vintage quilts and blocks. Her workmanship and creativity are awesome.

My amazing machine quilter, Becky Kraus, made everything run smoother. In addition to doing beautiful work, she is flexible and easy to work with—not easy when you're dealing with a crazed author who needed something yesterday. Becky also contributed the flag quilt.

Thank you to Chuck Brandt, my stepbrother, for lending me Dad's quilt, and to my niece, Paige Magley, for lending me the pillow that features her grandparents (my parents), Joan and Carl Brandt.

Thank you to Judy Pray, my editor at Stonesong Press. Judy is organized and thorough and has done a wonderful job. It has truly been a pleasure to work with her.

Thank you, too, to Alison Brown Cerier at Creative Publishing. She has always been willing to listen and work through problems, questions, and concerns. It has been a pleasure to work with her, too.

Thank you to Paul Fargis of Stonesong Press for asking me to write this book. It has been a joy to put my memories into quilts.

And, finally, thank you to my mother-in-law Dee Bickley, for providing my family with so many special memories. Born Antonietta Scarcia in Pietracamela, Italy, Dee was raised in the coal-mining town of Saxton, Pennsylvania, where she was the oldest of eleven children. She and her husband Jim raised their own family of four children all over the world. My husband John is their youngest child.

Dee is a woman with boundless energy and enthusiasm. She always looks at life as an adventure and at problems as opportunites, not obstacles. After years of walking everywhere she could, Dee started running in marathons (yes, that's 26.2 miles) in her seventies. She held the U.S. record in her age group for the 10-mile race in her eighties. She ran her last marathon when she was eighty-four.

Dee has been a part of our lives on so many occasions, always creating wonderful memories in the process. On a trip to Italy to visit Dee's birthplace, she beat two young men up the many, many steps to the very top of St. Peters Cathedral in Rome. My daughter overheard the young men when they reached the top, somewhat winded, say that they were passed up on the stairs by a little white-haired old lady. My daughter turned to them and said proudly, "That was my grandmother!"

Thank you, Dee, for the many ways you have shared your life and your enthusiasm with us. Thank you for being a wonderful inspiration to your family. And, of course, thank you for the memories. They will be part of our lives forever.